John Brown, Patrick Hutchison

The Absurdity and Perfidy of All Authoritative Toleration of Gross Heresy, Blasphemy, Idolatry, Popery

in two letters to a friend, in which the doctrine of the Westminster confession of faith relative to toletration of a false religion

John Brown, Patrick Hutchison

The Absurdity and Perfidy of All Authoritative Toleration of Gross Heresy, Blasphemy, Idolatry, Popery

in two letters to a friend, in which the doctrine of the Westminster confession of faith relative to toletration of a false religion

ISBN/EAN: 9783337090623

Printed in Europe, USA, Canada, Australia, Japan

Cover: Foto ©Lupo / pixelio.de

More available books at **www.hansebooks.com**

The ABSURDITY *and* PERFIDY *of all autho-ritative*

TOLERATION

OF

Grofs Herefy, Blafphemy, Idolatry, Popery, in BRITAIN.

IN TWO LETTERS TO A FRIEND.

IN WHICH

The Doctrine of the Weftminfter Confeffion of Faith relative to Toleration of a Falfe Religion, and the power of the Civil Magiftrate about Sacred Matters; and the Nature, Origin, Ends and Obligation of the National Covenant and Solemn League are candidly reprefented and defended.

BY JOHN BROWN,
Minifter of the Gofpel in HADDINGTON.

GLASGOW:

Printed by JOHN BRYCE;
And Sold by the Bookfellers in Town and Country.

M,DCC,LXXX.

LETTER I.

On the abſurdity of *Authoritative* TOLERATION of *groſs Hereſy, Blaſphemy* or *Idolatry*.

SIR,

HOW God himſelf connected religion, and the civil welfare of nations, in his ancient laws, almoſt the whole of the Old Teſtament doth bear witneſs. That religion is the great baſis of civil happineſs, was the common, the avowed belief of every ſenſible Heathen : It was, for ought I know, the infamous monſter Tiberius, who firſt pretended, *That the Gods alone ought to regard or reſent the injuries done them*. Before the happy Reformation, the Popiſh clergy had reduced civil rulers into mere tools for executing their pleaſure in religious matters; and pretended that they *had no power of judging* in them. To free theſe rulers from ſuch Antichriſtian claims, the Proteſtant reformers, every where, as their Confeſſions of faith and other writings make evident, loudly maintained, That to magiſtrates themſelves independent of clergymen, belongs a diſtinguiſhed power in the *reformation* and *preſervation* of religion. Not long after, Eraſtus, a German phyſician and his followers, to curry favour with their reſpective princes, pretended, That magiſtrates are the proper lords of the Chriſtian church, from whom her miniſters and other rulers derive their whole power, and to whom they muſt be accountable. This notion, exceedingly flattering their ambition, was too greedily embraced by moſt of the Proteſtant princes; nor do I know of one Proteſtant church, which hath not ſuffered by
means

means of it. Meanwhile, the German Anabaptists, having experienced the frowns, and sometimes the improper severities of magistrates, copied after the ancient Donatists in the like circumstances, and warmly contended, That magistrates have no more power about religious matters than any private person, and ought to punish none for different sentiments in doctrine or forms of worship. The Socinians and remonstrant Arminians, except when magistrates favoured themselves, and promoted their cause, zealously contended for the same notion, at least in the case of ministers and worship, which were not maintained at the public expence. Many, if not most of the English Independents in the last century were much of the same mind; and hence, by their influence, some passages in the Westminster Confession of Faith could never obtain a ratification by the English Parliament, or a place in their own *Savoy Confession*. Part of these passages, relative to the magistrate's power, are also dropt from the Confession of Faith agreed to by the Independents of New England in 1682. Most of the English Dissenters of this century seem to be much of the same mind; especially such as might otherwise have been exposed to danger on account of their open maintenance of Arian, Socinian, and Quakerish blasphemies —Locke and bishop Hoadly, and some others of the Episcopalian party, warmly espoused the same cause.

This notion never received much countenance in Scotland, till Mr Glass of Tealing commenced a furious new-fashioned Independent. He mightily contended, That the Jewish nation was an ecclesiastical one, and their kings ecclesiastical rulers; that Christian magistrates have no more power in religious matters than private Christians, and ought not to employ their power in advancing the true religion, or in making laws with penalties in favour of it; or in restraining or punishing heretics or false teachers, nor ought they to give more encouragement to good Christians, than to other peaceable subjects;—that the example of the reforming kings of Judah in punishing idolatry and false worship, and in promoting the true religion, is not now to be imitated; and that our fathers national covenan-

covenanting against Popery and other wickedness, in favour of the true religion was *unwarrantable*, and is *not binding* upon us.—— *Dr. Wishcart, Principal of the college of Edinburgh*, in his sermons contended, That magistrates have only a right to punish such crimes as strike immediately against the persons or property of men; but not to punish any thing which strikes immediately against the honour of God, as blasphemy or heresy; that all men ought to have civil liberty to think and speak as they please, providing they make no attack upon the welfare of civil society; that none ought to be hampered in their search after truth by any requirement of their subscriptions to *Formulas* or *Confessions of Faith*; that children in their education, ought never to be biassed to a side by learning catechisms which maintain the peculiar principles of a party. These or the like notions have been adopted by not a few of the pretenders to modern illumination.

In her *public Standards*, the Church of Scotland hath renounced, and in her solemn covenants hath abjured both these extremes. In her Old *Confession of Faith*, which is expresly sworn to in the national covenant of 1581, &c. as *in all points the undoubted truth of God*, Art. xxiv. she asserts, that " the power and authority of magistrates is God's *holy ordinance*, ordained for manifestation of his own glory, and for the singular profit of mankind——they are the *lieutenants of God*, in whose sessions God himself doth sit and judge——to whom by God is given the sword to the praise and defence of good men, and to punish all open malefactors. To kings, princes, rulers and magistrates chiefly, and most principally, the conservation and purgation of religion appertains; so that not only are they appointed for civil policy, but also for maintenance of the true religion, and for suppression of all idolatry and superstition whatsoever." This doctrine is further asserted and explained in her second book of discipline, chap. ix; The doctrine of her *Westminster Confession of Faith*, the WHOLE of which is solemnly espoused and engaged to, by every Presbyterian minister and elder in Scotland in his ordination vows, is that " for their publishing opinions or main-

taining practices contrary to the light of nature and the known principles of Christianity, whether concerning faith, worship or conversation, or to the power of godliness, or such erroneous opinions or practices, as either, in their own nature, or in the manner of publishing and maintaining them, are destructive to the external peace, and order, which Christ hath established in the church, they may be lawfully called to account, and proceeded against by—the power of the civil magistrate," Chap. xx. 4.—that "God, the supreme Lord and King of all the world, hath ordained civil magistrates to be under him, over the people, for his own glory and the public good—they ought especially, (in managing their office) to maintain PIETY, justice and peace, according to the *wholesome* laws of each commonwealth ——That the civil magistrate—HATH authority, and it is his duty to take order that unity and peace be preserved in the church, and that the truth of God be kept pure and entire; that all blasphemies and heresies be suppressed, all corruptions and abuses in worship and discipline prevented and reformed, and all the ordinances of God duly settled, administered and observed. For the better effecting of which, he hath power to call Synods, to be present at them, and to provide that whatsoever is transacted in them be according to the mind of God," Chap. xxiii. 1, 2, 3.——" The duties required in the second commandment are—the disapproving, detesting, opposing all false worship, and according to each one's place and calling, removing it, and all monuments of idolatry;——The sins forbidden in the second commandment are, all devising, counselling, commanding, using, and any ways approving any religious worship not instituted by God himself, tolerating a false religion." Lar. Cat. Q 108, 109. These declarations are an authentic explication of the power of the magistrate in *maintaining and preserving the true religion*, the defence of which is expresly sworn in their solemn covenants with God. If therefore, Sir, you discredit this doctrine, and plead the toleration of idolatry, blasphemy, heresy, and that magistrates ought to meddle with nothing in religion, be so honest, as openly to renounce your ordination vows and
the

the Confession of Faith and Catechisms, as well as the national Covenant and Solemn League.

To illustrate the above doctrine of our excellent standards, it is proper to observe, (1.) God alone is the necessarily existent, and absolutely independent Creator and preserver, and therefore original and supreme proprietor and governor of all things in heaven or earth, Exod. iii. 4 Gen. i. Psal. civ. and xxiv. 1, 2. xxxiii. 6. lxxxiii. 18. xlvii. 2, 7, 9. Ezek. i. 11. Col. i. 16,—18. Dan. iv. 34, 35. (2.) All right, civil, natural, or spiritual, whether of conscience, or of persons, or of husbands, parents, masters, magistrates, ministers, or even of Christ as mediator, must therefore wholly originate from God alone, Psalm cxv. 16. Rom. ii. 36. Heb. ii. 10 Acts x. 25, 28. 2 Cor. v. 18. Psal. lxxv. 7. Dan. ii. 21. iv. 32, 35. Mat. xxviii. 18. ii. 27 John v. 35. To suppose any real right or being whatsoever, unoriginating from him, is to give up with the necessary existence of God, and to plunge into the very *depths of Atheism.* (3.) All right and authority of conscience, persons, husbands, parents, magistrates, ministers, or even of Christ as mediator, being wholly derived from God, ought, necessarily ought, wholly to be improved, or exercised in his name, in conformity and subordination to his law, as the supreme rule, and in order to promote his declarative glory as the chief end of it, Prov. xvi. 4 Rom ii. 30. 1 Pet. iv. 11. 1 Cor x. 31. John v. 30. viii. 29 vii. 18. Eph iii. 21 (4.) No right or authority derived from God can therefore be lawfully improven or exercised, in protecting, encouraging, allowing or commanding any thing which God himself, on account of his infinite-perfection in holiness, justice, goodness and truth, cannot command; ---or in discouraging, disallowing, or prohibiting any thing which God in his law requires. It is absurd to suppose it, that God can give men a power which he hath not himself; and shocking blasphemy to suppose him capable of giving men a right and authority to contemn or counteract his own law as their rule, or his own glory as their chief end, in every thing they do, 2 Tim. ii. 13. Hab. i 12, 13. Exod. xv. 11. Deut. xxxii. 4. Zeph. iii. 5. James i. 13. (5.) All the diversified forms of right and authority in conscience, husbands, parents, masters, magistrates, ministers, and even in Christ as mediator, being derived from the *same God of infinite wisdom and order*, each of them may, and ought to be wholly exercised within its proper department, and in a manner answerable to its nature, and never in the way of invading the place or interrupting the exercise of any other right or authority. No right of conscience can be exercised to the interruption of the due exercise of marital, parental, magisterial, magistratical, ministerial, or Christ's mediatorial authority; nor, can any regular exercise of these powers interrupt the due exercise of the power of conscience, or of one another, 1 Cor. xiv. 33, 40. vii. 20, 24. (6.) All these different forms of power and authority being derived from the *same God*, may have the same things for their object, but viewed in different respects. The same man may be subject to the power of his conscience as he is a rational creature,---subject to the power of parents as a child,---subject to the power of masters as a servant,---subject to the power of magistrates as a member of the commonwealth,---subject to the power of church rulers as a member of an organized visible church,---subject to the mediatorial power of Christ, as a member of his mystical body, or an agent for promoting the welfare of it.------The same good work of piety or virtue may, or ought to be required by conscience, by parents, masters, magistrates, ministers, and even by Christ as mediator, in different respects, as calculated to promote the welfare of the persons, families, nations, and churches concerned,---in subordination to the glory of God as their respective proprietor and superior. The performance of the same good work may be encouraged by rewards from all these different powers, answerable to their respective forms.----- The same vices of idolatry, blasphemy, calumny, treason, theft, murder, &c. as in different respects hurtful to persons, families, civil societies, and churches, may, and ought to be prohibited by all these different powers, and resented by each, as hurtful to itself, as subordinated to God,---in a manner answerable to its particular nature and department,---by conscience with stinging rebukes,---by parents with correction, disinheriting,

heriting, or the like, - by masters with frowns, stripes, abridgment of wages, or the like, - by magistrates with public dishonour, fining, imprisonment, or death,--- by church rulers with ecclesiastical rebuke, excommunication,-- by Christ with temporal, spiritual or eternal judgment, Acts xxiv. 16. Josh xxiv. 15. Psal. ci. Mat. v, vi, vii, &c. (7.) All these powers of conscience, husbands, parents, masters, magistrates, church rulers, and of Christ as mediator, proceeding from an infinitely wise, powerful and good God, are each of them, in its own place, altogether sufficient to gain its own end.---Nevertheless, it mightily tends to the advantage of each, that all of them be rightly exercised at once, and to the hurt of all the rest, if any of them be not. If conscience act faithfully, this promotes the regular and comfortable exercise of the power of husbands, parents, masters, magistrates or ministers, &c. And it is to the advantage of conscience, if they regularly exercise their power, and especially if Christ exercise his, in a remarkable manner. It is much to the advantage of Church and State, if husbands, parents, and masters, faithfully exercise their power in their respective departments; and much to their hurt, if they do not. If the rulers in Church and State, faithfully discharge their trust, it will tend much to promote the welfare of families. The more faithfully ministers labour in winning souls to Christ, and teaching men to live soberly, righteously and godly in view of Christ's second coming, the more easy will the work of magistrates, and the greater the happiness of the commonwealth be.——The more faithfully magistrates act in curbing of crimes, and promoting obedience to God the King of nations, as a mean of securing his felicitating blessing to the commonwealth, the more delightfully will church-power be exercised, and the more abundantly it will tend to the welfare of the church. Nay, though the mediatorial power of Christ be infinitely sufficient in its own place, to answer its own ends, yet the delightful exercise and success of it is not a little promoted by the faithful exercise of the powers of conscience, husbands, parents, masters, magistrates and church-rulers, Acts xxiv. 16. 1 Tim. i. 5. Eph. iv,--vi. Col. iii.

iii. iv. 1 & 2 Tim. Titus i.---iii. 1 Pet. ii.---v. Pſalm ii. 10,- 12. Rev. ii. 15. xvii. 14, 16. xxi. 24. Iſa. xlix. 23. lx, 3, 4, 10, 16. (8.) Though the marital, parental, magiſterial, magiſtratical, and miniſterial powers be altogether diſtinct from, and independent of one another, and each of them have its own particular exerciſes pertaining to it alone ;-- yet the ſame perſon, in reſpect of different relations, may be at once ſuperior or inferior to another perſon,---and ſo may be required to fulfil the particular duties of his ſtation, by one who hath not any lawful right to perform them himſelf. Thus magiſtrates and miniſters as ſuch, may require huſbands to perform their duties to their wives, parents to perform theirs to their children, or maſters theirs to their ſervants, as a mean of promoting the welfare of the commonwealth and of the church, in obedience to God, and aiming at his glory. An uncrowned huſband of a queen may command her, faithfully to exerciſe her magiſtratical power, as a means of honour and happineſs to his family ; and ſhe as queen may command him in every thing relating to the welfare of the ſtate, as her officer or ſubject. A parent may require his ſon, as ſuch, faithfully to exerciſe his miniſterial, magiſtratical, or magiſterial power as a mean of honour and happineſs to his family. A ſon may command his father, who is his ſervant, in every thing pertaining to the ſervice due from him, and even to order his family aright, in ſo far as it tends to promote that ſervice. Miniſters, as the ambaſſadors of Chriſt, have power to require magiſtrates, *as church-members,* faithfully to exerciſe their magiſtratical power, ſo as may beſt promote the honour of Chriſt, and the welfare of his church. And on the other hand, magiſtrates have power to require miniſters *as their ſubjects,* faithfully to exerciſe their miniſterial power, as a mean of rendering the nation pious and virtuous, in order to promote its happineſs,---and all this in ſubordination to the law, and to promote the glory of God as the ſupreme governor of families, churches, or nations. (9.) Though the marital, parental, magiſterial, magiſtratical and miniſterial powers, have, each of them,

ſome-

something for its peculiar and distinguishing object, in which no other power can interfere with it;---Thus it is always unlawful for husbands, parents, masters or ministers, *as such*, to assume the power of civil magistrates in levying taxes, adjudging criminals to death,---always unlawful for parents, masters, or magistrates, *as such*, to preach the gospel, dispense sacraments, or church-censures;——yet if the exercise of some of these powers be fearfully neglected or abused, the other powers may be exercised, in order to rectify the disorders occasioned, further than would be proper if there were no such neglect, abuse, or disorder. Thus if husbands, parents, or masters, fearfully abuse their power, relative to wives, children, or servants, the rulers of church or state, for the benefit of these societies, may interfere more with their family-concerns, than would be proper in other circumstances. If church-rulers be notoriously negligent or wicked, magistrates *as church-members, and to promote the welfare of the state*, may do more in the reformation of the church, than would be proper for them, if church rulers were diligent and faithful. And, if through the indolence or wickedness of magistrates, the affairs of the nation be thrown into terrible confusion, ministers *as members of the commonwealth, and to promote the welfare of the church*, may do more in the rectification of affairs, than would be proper, if the magistrates were faithful, 2 Kings xi. 2 Chron. xxiii (10.) All governing authority empowers the possessors of it, to issue forth laws or commandments, binding on the subject of it. But these laws or commandments can extend their binding force no further, than the particular department belonging to that power, as by that, every particular form of authority, derived from God, is limited. The laws or commandments of parents, masters, magistrates, and church-rulers, extend only to external things in the family, commonwealth, or church. Those of conscience and of Christ extend also to that which is inward in the heart.---And as all human superiors are imperfect in knowledge themselves, and cannot enable their subjects perfectly to understand their whole duty, it is necessary that laws of families or nations, or constitutions of churches require *nothing but what is plainly agreeable to the law of God*, and nothing in religion but what is *plainly required by the word of God*, that so nothing may be contrary to these laws but what is not only *really*, but *plainly* contrary to the word of God. And, the weaker the subjects are, the more condescension ought to be exercised towards them in this matter, Rom. xv, 1, 2. (11.) As men cannot bow the hearts of their inferiors unto subjection, they ought always to issue forth their commandments in the most prudent, mild and gaining manner. It is very improper to issue forth any law doubtful or obscure, or which most of the subjects are not likely to be got peaceably to comply with. This ought especially to be attended to, in the framing and imposing of *laws and constitutions relative to religion*, which ought to be a *reasonable* and *voluntary* service. (12) As nothing, particularly in religion, ought to be contrary to any law of church or state but what is plainly contrary to the law of God; and nothing ought to be held *censurable* by the laws of the church, or *punishable* by the laws of the state, but what is *plainly contrary* to these laws, and hath become *duly public*, in the providence of God, without requiring the party concerned to be his own accuser.—So, on account of the weakness or number of the offenders, or the disordered state of the society, *many real scandals* in the church must be forborne without censure, and *many real crimes* against the state forborne without punishment; notwithstanding, it would be extremely wicked, *authoritatively* to license or tolerate them in either. If your children be very young, raving in a fever, delirious, or apt to fall into convulsive fits, it might be very prudent and dutiful for you to forbear severe chastisement of them for playing on the Lord's day; repeating some wicked expressions, they had heard from their fellow children, or the like. But would it be lawful in you to give them a parental licence to profane the Sabbath or name of God, and promise them protection in so doing? You dare not pretend it. God himself wisely forbears the punishment of many things, which his law forbids. (13.) As it is never errors or corruptions *of the heart*, but wick-

ed

ed words and deeds, sufficiently and regularly manifested, which are to be corrected in families, punished in commonwealths, or censured in churches, Deut. xiii. 1,---14. xvii. 46. Heb. x. 28. 1 Tim. v. 1.—So even in punishing manifest crimes, especially in matters of religion, all proper mildness ought to be exercised, never proceeding to extremities, where there is any hope of reformation, or where, as in the case of heresy or blasphemy, confession and repentance can make any kind of restitution, Mat. xviii. 15,--18. Among the Hebrews, not one appears to have been punished for idolatry, if he professed repentance and reformation. The princes of Israel first attempted to bring the Reubenites and Gadites, whom they supposed guilty of it, to repentance, Josh. xxii. Never in the reformation by Asa, Hezekiah, or Josiah, have we one instance of a penitent idolater slain. The idolaters condemned to death, Deut. xiii. xvii. are represented as *men of Belial*, presumptuous, and obstinate in their wickedness. The prophets of Baal whom Elijah caused be put to death, 1 Kings xviii. 40. and Mattan the priest, who was slain by Jehoiada's orders, 2 Kings xi. 18. were no doubt of this sort; and probably also guilty of promoting the murder of the Lord's prophets and people. The man put to death for profanation of the Sabbath, appears to have acted presumptuously, Num xv. 30,—36. Asa and his subjects covenanted to put to death such as obstinately adhered to idolatry, 2 Chron. xv. 12, 13. (14.) Magistrates ought never to attempt *forcing* men to believe with their hearts, even the most fundamental truths of religion, or to practise any religious duty,—that being no means appointed by God for convincing them of the truth, or inducing them to a cordial performance of religious duties, 2 Cor. x. 4, 5. But it would be highly absurd, hence to infer, That magistrates *may not restrain* men from robbing nations or churches of those divine truths, which God hath graciously entrusted to them, and which are inexpressibly profitable to them,—or *restrain* them from propagating gross heresies, blasphemies, idolatries, which undermine and exclude the true religion, provoke God to destroy nations, and are the fruitful seeds of contention, confusion, and every evil work. No magistrate can compel me to love my neighbour as myself, or can justly compel me to divide mine inheritance with him; but he may lawfully punish me for calumniating or robbing him.

It is, therefore, extremely uncandid in the advocates for magistratical tolerations of heresy, blasphemy, and idolatry, always to attempt blending or placing on an equal level, *true* and *false* religion,—*mere neglect* of some positive duties of religion, and *shocking insults* upon, and *opposition* to the duties of religion,—*lesser* and *secret mistakes* in religion, and the *most damnable* heresies, blasphemies, and idolatries, openly and obstinately professed and practised, as if these were equally objects of toleration, restraint, or punishment, —or, to confound a *mere forbearance* to punish, with an *authoritative licence*, openly to profess and practise what is criminal respecting religion. The true religion ought never to need a toleration. It ought always to have an establishment. Whereas a false one ought never to be established, magistrates having no power against the truth but for the truth. There are *many mere neglects* or *lesser mistakes* in religion, against which it would not be proper for magistrates to enact civil laws, in this present state of imperfection. And, if there be no civil law against them, they cannot be punishable as crimes. "Where no law is, there can "be no transgression."—Mere forbearance to punish, what is plainly contrary to law, is, in some cases, necessary, and in imitation of God himself; and gives no positive encouragement to wickedness. Whereas a *positive* or *authoritative* toleration, proclaims to men, a liberty to sin, and promiseth them protection in so doing. If the provider for an army deliver to them fine flour mixed with some particles of bran, and a large quantity of arsenic, Is his delivery of the fine flour, or even of the mixture of bran, as criminal and punishable, as that of the mixture of arsenic? No man that is not mad will pretend it. For the fine flour he deserves the highest *encouragement:* for the bran he may be justly *forborne;* but for the arsenic he deserves to be *hanged.*

The

The toleration, which I mean to oppose, if plainly and candidly expressed, would run thus: "We, the "King and Parliament of ————, as *powers or-* "*dained of God,*—*ministers of God for good* to men,— "as the *ordinance of God* for the *terror* and *punishment* "*of evil doers,* and the *praise of them that do well,*— "as *nursing fathers* to the church of Christ,—in or- "der that all our subjects may *come to the knowledge* "*of the truth,* and *lead a quiet and peaceable life in all* "*godliness and honesty*——Do hereby, in the *name* "*and authority* of The Most High GOD, from whom "we have derived all that governing power, which "we possess, that we, *ruling in his fear,* may exercise "it wholly in obedience to his law, and to promote "his declarative glory in the world—Grant to all and "every one of you, our said subjects, an *authorita-* "*tive toleration* or legal licence,—openly and obsti- "nately to pervert, contradict, and revile the decla- "rations of God contained in his word,—and in the "most insolent and abusive manner to blaspheme "his nature, perfections, purposes and works, par- "ticularly of the redemption of mankind,—and "to corrupt his worship, represent him in it, in the "most absurd and abominable forms,—or rob him of "it, giving it to devils, monsters of wickedness, "brutes, stocks, or stones, in his stead,—and with "all your might to exert yourselves, in making your "fellow subjects do the like.——And, we hereby do, "In *the same name and authority* of God, the King of "nations, promise you every kind and degree of ci- "vil protection in all such behaviour, as you can pro- "fess, or pretend, your consciences do dictate or al- "low,—providing always, that you commit your out- "rage only against God, your, and our Maker and "Sovereign,—but do not disturb the external peace "of the nation, in reviling the civil character, seizing "or hurting the civil property, or any way abusing "the body of any of your fellow sinners of mankind."
——The correspondent warrant of conscience which we mean to impugn, if honestly expressed, would run thus: "I Conscience, as the *great deputy* "of The Most High GOD, Lord, and Lawgiver "of the world, implanted in every man's breast, for

his

" his temporal, spiritual, and eternal advantage, Do
" hereby, *In God's name and authority*, and in the ex-
" ercife of my power which is wholly derived from
" him, and to be exercifed for his glory, in *trying all*
" *things by his law*, and *approving* and *holding faſt that*
" *which is good,*—Warrant and authorize all and eve-
" ry one of you, fons and daughters of men, to de-
" vife, believe, openly and obſtinately profefs, and
" zealoufly propagate every damnable herefy, and
" blafphemous opinion, and to practife and propa-
" gate every abfurd and abominable form of idolatry,
" which Satan, who deceiveth the world, and a
" heart deceitful above all things and defperately wick-
" ed, and given up of God to ſtrong delufion, belief
" of lies, vile affections, and a reprobate fenfe, can
" make you think innocent or proper.——And, I
" do hereby, In the *fame name and authority*,—Grant
" *you my facred claim of right* to all manner of liberty
" and protection from the civil magiſtrate in fo do-
" ing,—providing always, that you commit fuch in-
" jury and outrage only againſt God, your infinitely
" excellent, high, and gracious Proprietor and Su-
" perior, and do no civil injury to the body, charac-
" ter, or property of your fellow creatures." Such
is indeed the toleration which many praife or plead
for; and this I proceed to impugn, by the following
arguments.

1. Mens pleadings for it do, all of them, neceffarily proceed on their adopting fuch *atheiſtical principles* as the following, (1.) Mens natural or civil rights to their property, liberty, profits and honours, are not originally derived from God,- and ought to protect them in their moſt outragious finning againſt him (2,) Mens confciences have a right and authority, underived from, and independent of God, by which it can warrant them to think and fpeak of, or act towards God, as infolently and blafphemoufly as they pleafe. (3) That, if the law of God be any rule to men; it is not fo, in refpect of any intrinfic meaning affixed to it by him, but merely as it is underſtood by every man, particularly in that which relates to their behaviour towards God. (4.) All men being ready to miſtake, we ought always to believe that our op-

ponents may have as just a view of the scriptures as ourselves, and never to condemn them for that which they do not own to be blasphemy, idolatry, or heresy. (5.) Magistrates right and authority to govern others, doth not originate in God as the Creator, Preserver, and King of nations, but in magistrates themselves, *or in their subjects;* and so may be exercised as they please, particularly in requiring or allowing their subjects to belie, blaspheme, or rob God. (6) Magistrates may be moral governors deputies or lieutenants, under God, without having any power or authority relating to religion, or his honour. (7.) Not the law of God natural or revealed, but the laws of nations ought to be the *supreme* standard of all civil government. (8.) Not the declarative glory of God, as the Most High over all the earth, but the civil peace and prosperity of nations, ought to be the *chief end* of magistrates in all their acts of government. (9) Mens natural rights of conscience, or their civil rights, or the authority of magistrates, may or ought to empower, warrant, or protect them in gross heresy, blasphemy, idolatry, or other outragious abuse and injury of God; but can by no means warrant or protect them in calumny, theft, murder, or any other injuries against men. (10.) There is no real difference between moral good and evil, at least in things pertaining to God; and so true and false religion are equally calculated to promote the welfare of civil society, and the virtues which render men good, peaceable, useful, and honourable rulers or subjects,—and hence heretics, blasphemers, and idolaters may be *good subjects.* (11.) The favour or indignation of God is of no importance to civil society; and therefore magistrates ought to use no means to procure his favour by the encouragement of true religion, or to avert his indignation by the restraint of gross heresy, blasphemy, or idolatry,—but only labour to procure the friendship of men, and prevent their injuring the character, property, or bodies of their subjects ——— That all these propositions are *really atheistical,* is manifest. They all give up with the necessary existence, infinite excellency, and absolute supremacy of God, without any of which, he cannot be God at all.——That Locke, Hoadly

Hoadly, Blackburn, Voltaire, and others, advocates for *authoritative toleration* of false religion, found their pleadings on the above propositions, is no less evident to every judicious and unbiassed observer.—Nay, did not modesty forbid, I might defy all the world to plead for *such toleration*, without taking all, or some of the above or like atheistical propositions for granted.

II. The scriptures plainly represent magistrates granting of men an unrestrained freedom to profess and practise a false religion as extremely sinful and hurtful. (1.) It is in the name of God to give a *liberty to the flesh*, of which *heresies* and *idolatry* are the manifest and damning works, Gal. v. 13, 19,—21. with Rom. viii, 7, 8. (2.) It is not merely to *pity* and *spare*, but to *encourage* such as seek to draw away their subjects from God, contrary to Deut. xiii. 9, 10. Eph. xiv. 14. 2 Tim. iii. 4, 5, 13. 2 Pet. ii. 1, 2, 3. (3.) In so doing, magistrates, as political shepherds, not only suffer the flock of God, the King of nations, under their charge, to *wander* or be *driven* from their fold and pasture, but encourage them in it,—contrary to Ezek. xxxiv. 5,—8. Acts xx. 30. (4.) It marks a heavy judgment of God upon, and an anarchy in a commonwealth, when every man is left without restraint, and doth that which is right in his own eyes, in matters of religion, Judges xvii. 6. Zech. xi. 9, 16. 2 Chron. xx. 33. Amos iv. 4, 5. (5.) In granting *such liberty*, magistrates are not for Christ, by whom they rule, Prov. viii. 15, 16. but against him, in encouraging and protecting the doctrines and works of the devil, which he came to destroy, John viii. 44. 1 Tim. iv. 2. Rev. xvi. 13, 14 with 1 John iii. 8. Zech. xiii. 2. (6) False religion eats out the true doctrine of Christ, and the true piety and virtue which proceed from the faith of it,—which are like joints and bands to connect and establish a nation, Isa. liii. 5. 2 Tim. ii. 16, 17. Gal. v. 10, 11, 12. (7.) Heresies produce *divisions*, 1 Cor. xi. 18, 19. make men *wanton*, *filthy dreamers*, *despisers* and *revilers* of magistrates, Jude, ver. 4, 8. 2 Pet. ii. 10,—17. they render times *perilous*, and make men *traitors*, *heady*, *high minded, truce-breakers, false accusers, fierce, without natural affection, despisers of those that are good,* 2 Tim iii. 1,—13. They produce *envy, strifes, evil surmisings,* and *perverse disputings,* 1 Tim. vi. 3, 4. Gal. v. 19, 20. they spoil Christ's vines, Song ii. 15. (8.) False religion deprives a nation of God's protecting hedge of favourable providence, and opens an inlet or the floods of destructive judgments, Exod. xxxii. 25. Ezek. xiii. 4, 5. and xxii. 30, 31. (9.) Magistrates indulgence of a false religion is represented as *a kicking at the true religion,* and *on honouring of the corrupters above God,* and brings a charge of the wickedness upon the tolerators of it. Hence Eli the judge of Israel is represented as *kicking at God's sacrifice, honouring his profane sons above God,* and *making himself fat* with God's portion of the sacrifices, because he did not effectually reform his sons, 1 Sam. ii. 12,—16, 23,—25, 29. Eph. v 7, 11. and Nehemiah contended with the rulers of Judah for suffering the worship of God to be neglected, and the Sabbath profaned, Neh. xiii. 10,—18. (10.) Such indulgence of false or corrupt religion is represented as tending to make men abhor the true religion, and speak evil of it, 1 Sam. ii. 17. 2 Pet. ii, 1,—3.

III. The scriptures represent magistrates as having power to make civil laws relative to the external concerns of religion subordinated to the law of God, and answerable to their own department. (1.) They have in charge the keeping of the whole law of God, Deut. xvii. 19. 1 Kings ii. 3. Josh. i. 7, 8. 2 Chron xxiii. 11. Job xxix. 25. Rom. xiii. 1,—4. It is never hinted, that they have no charge with respect to religion, but the contrary. God chose Moses the magistrate, not Aaron the High-priest to publish his laws relative to religion.——Abijah avers, that in maintaining the true worship of God, he had kept the charge of the Lord, which Jeroboam the introducer of a false religion had not, 2 Chron xiii. 10, 11. (2.) God promised to the Jews good magistrates, in order to root out abusive practices and monuments of false religion, Isa i. 25, 26. Now, if they had power to root these out, they had certainly power to make laws for that effect. (3.) They ought to repeal wicked and persecuting

cuting laws, and free their subjects from being bound over to punishment by them for their faithful service of God, Psalm xciv. 20. Isa. x. 11. Mic. vi. 16. Hof. v. 11. If they can repeal wicked laws, they must have power to establish what is contrary to them, Dan. iii. and vi. (4.) If magistrates can make laws encouraging the true religion and church of Christ, by annexation of civil favours to the profession or practice of gospel-truth; they can also by law annex civil punishment to the contempt of, or rebellion against these laws; they being for the *terror and punishment of evil doers*, as well as for the *praise of them that do well*, Rom. xiii. 3, 4. 1 Pet. ii. 13, 14 Dan. vi. 16 iii. 29. Ezra i. 1,—5. vi. 3,—12. vii. 23,—27. (5) By enacting such laws they neither invade the office of ecclesiastical rulers, who have no power to connect civil rewards or punishments, with any thing religious, —nor do they transgress any law of God.——What then can hinder their having power to make them? (6.) If all sorts of men, church members and officers, as well as others, be subject to civil magistrates, they must have power, and ought to make civil laws calculated to promote their advantage, in all these stations, Rom. xiii. 1,—4. 1 Pet. ii. 13, 14. 1 Tim. ii 1, 2. (7.) Unless magistrates have a power to make good laws relative to the external profession and practice of religion, clergymen, if generally corrupt, will have it in their power, by Synodical constitutions, or otherwise, to devour and poison their subjects, with the seeds of confusion, profaneness, and every evil work, without any possibility of any legal restraint. For to allow magistrates to act without law, is to introduce tyranny and arbitrary government.

But, in magistrates making laws respecting religion, it is necessary, that [1.] They, first in order, carefully acquaint themselves with the law of God, that they may form all their laws in agreeableness and subordination to it,—they having no power against the truth, but for it, Deut. xvii. 18,—20. Josh. i. 7, 8. Psalm cxix. 97,—104. 2 Cor. xiii. 8 [2.] They ought to consult with faithful ministers of the church, either as met in Synods or otherwise; as it may be expected, they know the laws of God relative to religion, Deut. xvii. 9, --12. Mal. ii. 7. 2 Chron. xv. 1, ---15 Thus, in making these laws, church-rulers help magistrates with their *direction*, while magistrates help them with their *civil encouragements*, 2 Chron. xix. 10, 11. Ezek. xliv. 23, 24 [3.] They ought to require the ministers, who are in their dominions, faithfully to instruct their subjects in the whole counsel of God, contained in his word, relative to those points of religion, about which they intend to make laws, that they may be thus prepared, *willingly* to receive and obey them.—Thus Jehoshaphat first sent *teachers*, and then *judges* throughout his dominions, 2 Chron. xvii xix [4.] In all matters of religion, great care ought to be taken to establish the laws, with and by, the consent of the subjects, or their representatives,—thus strengthening these laws, through their binding men who are *willing* to obey them ;— and the rather as the principal end of such laws is lost, unless men willingly obey them, 2 Chron. xv. 9, 13. xx. 21. Jonah iii 4, 7. [5.] In these laws a special regard ought to be shewn to persons of a weak and tender conscience. Political shepherds ought never to over drive their flock, but to carry the lambs in their bosom. And, that the very weakest of their subjects may be qualified to obey their laws, they ought never to establish any thing in religion, but what is *plainly* as well as *really* established by God in his law ; —that so nothing may be contrary to their law, but what is plainly contrary to God's law, Ezek. xxxiv. 4.

IV. Though the law of God allows not of magistrates attempting to *force* men into the faith, profession or practice of the true religion, or of their punishing any thing relative to it, which is not an open and manifest violation of the law of God, and plainly destructive of the welfare of the commonwealth ;—yet it requires them to *restrain*, and even *seasonably* and *suitably* to *punish* blasphemy, idolatry, and like grosser corruptions, and insults upon the true religion, when they become openly notorious, and especially if obstinately continued in to the just offence and hurt of others. (1) Such *restraint* and *punishment* are represented in scripture as an eminent service done to God, Exod. xxxii. 4, 26, 29. 1 Sam. xv. 2, 3. xviii 22.

Rev.

Rev. xvii. 14, 16. xix. 17,---19. Song ii. 15 in which last text, the word rendered TAKE ordinarily signifies an external and forcible taking, compare 2 Sam. i. 10. Judges xii. 6. xvi 3, 21. Psalm cxxxix. 9 Exod. iv. 4. Gen. xxv. 26. xxii. 13. (2.) The end of God's appointment of magistrates, is the GOOD of the subjects, Rom. xiv. 4. Now such corruptions in religion impair *that good;* in preventing the spread and success of the gospel, which are so exceedingly calculated to render men virtuous and happy, even in this life, 1 Tim. iv. 8. 1 Pet. iii. 11, 12, 13. Tit. ii. 12. and in promoting the hurt of mens morals, safety, estate, peace or liberty, Rom. i. 21,—32. xvi. 18. 2 Pet. ii. 1, 2, 3, 10, 12, 13, 16, 18, 19. Jude, ver 4, 8, 10, 11, 12, 13, 16, 18, 19. 2 Tim. iv. 3, 4. iii. 1,—9, 13. ii. 16, 17. 1 Tim. iv. 2,---5. vi. 3, 4. (3) Such restraint and punishment are represented in scripture as a *blessing* to be prayed for, 1 Tim. ii. 1, 2, 4. and as a *blessing* for which God ought to be thanked, Ezra vii. 25---28 Rev. xi. 15, 17. (4.) It is promised, that such restraint and punishment should be produced by the effusion of the holy Ghost upon the Christian church, Zech xii. 10, 12, 14. with xiii. 1---6. and that they should tend to the advantage, even of some seducers, who should be brought to account the inflicters their real FRIENDS, Zech. xiii. 4, 5, 6. (5) The scripture represents EVIL as removed, and GOOD both moral and civil as obtained, by such restraints and punishments, Deut. xvii. 2, 5, 7, 10. 1 Kings xviii. 40, 41 2 Chron. xiv. 3, 4, 5. and wickedness and misery as overflowing a nation, when neglected, Eccl. viii. 11. Judg. xvii. 4, 5, 6, 12 1 Sam. ii. 12,---29 and iv. Ezek. xxii 25, 26, 30, 31. (6.) When the proper judges neglected such restraint and punishment, God raised up some in an extraordinary way, to execute it. Thus Elijah caused slay the prophets of Baal, 1 Kings xviii. 40. Jehu caused slay others of them, 2 Kings x. 5,---25 The Jews, under the direction of Jehoiada, slew Mattan the priest of Baal, and Christ himself once and again drove the buyers and sellers out of the temple, John ii. 13,--19. Mat. xxi. 12. Why ought not magistrates, who are

his

his vicegerents, as God, to imitate his conduct, Psal. lxxxii. 1, 6.- 2 Chron. xix. 6. Rom. xiii. 1,---4. (7.) The scripture affords many approven instances of such restraint or punishment of gross corruptions in religion, as by Jacob, Gen. xxxv 24. by the judges in the time and country of Job, Job xxxi. 26,---28. by Moses, Exod. xxxii. 4, 20, 22, 29. by the rulers of the ten tribes, Josh. xxii, 10,---34. by Asa, 2 Chron. xv. 12, 13, 15. by Jehoshaphat, 2 Chron. xix. 3,---8. by Josiah, 2 Chron. xxxiv. 4, 33, 2 Kings xxiii. 5, 20. by Nehemiah, Neh. x. 20. by Nebuchadnezzar, Dan. iii. 29. by Artaxerxes, Ezra vii. 26. and by the Protestant destroyers of Antichrist, Rev. xvii. 16.

V. Beside their power, as men, to try all things by the law of God manifested to them, and their power of Christian discretion (if they are Christians) to judge by the word of God what is for their own spiritual and eternal advantage, magistrates, as such, have a power of POLITICALLY judging and determining, what and how, principles and practices of *the true religion* are to be connected with political rewards or encouragements; or, what ought to be professed and practised by persons, as members of their political society, in order to promote the real welfare of it, in subordination to the glory of God, as King of nations. - (1) If they may enact laws in the matters of God, as hath been proven; and may judge in what is fundamental in religion,---or in that which is contained in express words of scripture,---or in matters of the second table of the moral law,-- then they must have power to judge of that which is plainly deducible from the express words of scripture, by necessary consequence,---and in those matters of the first table of the moral law, which as much belong to the law of nature, as any in the second ;——have power politically to judge why, and how, such a religious profession and practice is to be encouraged by the civil authority ; and how, and why, that which is notoriously opposite to the true religion, is to be discouraged. (3.) Without this *political* judging of them, magistrates could never determine, Whether the decisions of ecclesiastical courts ought to be ratified by their civil authority or not, 1 Thess. v. 21. Acts xvii. 11.

in judging of those things, magistrates improve the Word, the Spirit, and the faithful ministers of God, for their counsellors, they bid fair to have a *divine sentence in their lips, and not to err in judgment*, Deut. xvii. 18,---20. Psal. cxix. 97,---105 Prov. xvi. 10. Isa. xxxii. 1. If, neglecting to consult these, magistrates give a corrupt sentence, they ly open to the judgment of God,-- to the restraint and correction of the collective body of the subjects, or their representatives,-- and also to ecclesiastical censure, if they be church-members. (3) If magistrates be *nursing fathers* to the Christian church, Isa. xlix. 23. they ought to prevent her being poisoned with corrupt food; and hence must have a power *politically* to judge what is corrupt, and what is not. (4.) If the magistrate be the keeper of the peace of the kingdom, then, if a party in the church, complaining of the gross errors of the other, should form a furious schism, he must have power *politically* to judge, who is in the right, or in the wrong.—who adhere to the truths established by law, and who do not ;—and to shew favour accordingly, 1 Thess. v. 21. (5) If magistrates may restrain and punish evil doers, they may exercise this power over church officers, if, in their Synods, they make blasphemous or idolatrous decrees, which tend to disturb the commonwealth, and dishonour God, the King of nations,—and hence must *politically* judge of their conduct by the laws of God and the land. ———No covenanted subjection to church judicatures, as a member of the church, can deprive them of this *political* judgment, any more than of their right of *cognition* and *discretion* as men and Christians. Magistrates *political* judgment, how principles or practices are to be connected with civil encouragements or discouragements, is no infallible rule of church courts judging, how principles and practices ought to be connected with ecclesiastical encouragements or censures: nor are the decisions of ecclesiastical courts any infallible rule to direct magistrates. But the law of God is the *only infallible* and *supreme* rule to both. Nor is the decision of the one *subordinate* to that of the other; but both, as well as every man's right to judge for himself according to the law of God, what he is to believe and practise in order to his own peace and comfort, and his joyful answering in the final judgment of God, are *supreme* in their respective departments, subordinated only to the judgment of God himself.——But, to argue the matter still more particularly,

1. If magistracy, conscience, and human rights, natural and civil, be all *derived from God*, as all but Atheists must allow, magistrates can have no more power, *authoritatively* to tolerate sin, than God himself can command it. If God, by virtue of the infinite perfection of his nature, have no will, no power, *authoritatively* to proclaim liberty to commit sin, he cannot communicate any such power to the magistrate. Nor can the magistrate account to God for exceeding his power in licensing that which is infinitely injurious to him, more than the British king's Lion-keeper hath power, or could be accountable for loosing and hunting out the lions in the Tower upon His Majesty. If conscience derive all its power from God, it can have no more power to enjoin any thing sinful, than Lord North hath to hire ruffians to assassinate his Sovereign. If all human rights be derived from God, the primary and supreme proprietor of all things, it is impossible they can *authorize* men to contrive or commit any thing sinful, or can *protect* them in it.

2. Mens state in this world is neither *separated* nor *separable* from, but closely connected with their eternal state. And magistracy is an *ordinance of God*, appointed by him for his own glory, and to promote the chief end of mankind in glorifying him, Rom. xiii. 2. Prov. xvi. 4. 1 Cor. x. 31. 1 Pet. iv. 11. Rom. xii. 36. But, how, Sir, do magistrates promote this end, if they give the same *degree of protection*, though perhaps, not of encouragement, to the soul-ruining and practice-corrupting delusions and abominations of Satan, as they do the eternally saving religion of God and his Christ?—if they give the same countenance to them, who to the corruption of mens moral behaviour, and their eternal damnation,—defame Jehovah to them as *mere matter*, a *mere man*, a *mere creature*, a *worker of contradiction and nonsense*,—as they do to those, who faithfully proclaim his infinite excellen's,

cellencies, and glorious works of redemption, publish his truths, and promote the present and future holiness and happiness of mankind?—If God chiefly aim at the glorifying of himself, in the advancement of the kingdom of Christ; how can magistrates, who are appointed by him, as his vicegerents, for promoting his glory on earth, be allowed, far less obliged by him, to exert their power, as much for protecting or promoting the kingdom of the devil, as for the advancement of the kingdom of Christ? Indeed magistrates are not the deputies of Christ as mediator, but they are of God, Father, Son and Holy Ghost, and all their administrations are, by him, subjected to Christ, as "Head over all things to his church," Prov. viii. 15, 16. Mat. xxviii. 18. Eph. i. 22. Why then ought they not to concur with God, in advancing the kingdom of Christ, especially as this mightily promotes the temporal as well as the eternal welfare of their subjects, Prov. xiv. 34. Isa. i. 19. iii. 10. Psal. cxii, cxxvii, cxxviii.

3. Magistrates are expresly represented in scripture, *as ministers of God for good to men,*—rulers deputed by, and under him, Rom. xiii. 4. But, how can they be *ministers, deputies,* or *vicegerents* of God, without having power to restrain, and *if proper* and *seasonable,* to punish, that which openly affronts and horridly insults him,—blasphemously gives him the lie, basely misrepresents him, or devotes the worship due to him, to his adversary the devil,—or any other crimes, which immediately strike against him?—If they be God's ministers, they must transact all their magistratical managements in his name,—and how can God empower *his own ministers* as such, and acting in his name, to promote his highest dishonour, licensing, encouraging, and protecting gross heresy, blasphemy, and idolatry;—giving as much encouragement to the vilest delusions of Satan, as to the new Testament in Jesus blood?—How can they be ministers of God for good to men, without having power to restrain such as, like wolves and murderers, go about corrupting the principles and practices, and destroying the sons of his and their subjects? How can they

they be ministers of God, the father of spirits, *for good, universal good,* to men, who are not brutes but endowed with precious and immortal souls, which are more beneficial in commonwealths, than their bodies, without having power to promote the cultivation and welfare of souls as a means of promoting the happiness of that state? How can they be ministers of God *for good to men,* if they have power, only to punish those crimes which strike immediately against their bodies or external property, but no power to punish crimes, as they provoke God's wrath against the nation;——if they have power to restrain the petty thief, robber, or other less hurtful things,—but none to prevent the kindling of God's wrath against the nation, and the debauching of mens consciences and morals, by blasphemy, heresy, idolatry, &c. which may quickly do more real mischief to a nation, than ten thousand thieves or robbers could do?——After God hath expresly commanded to punish murderers as *destroyers of his image,* Gen. ix. 6.—have his ministers no power to punish murder, as a destruction of his rational creatures, or a sacrificing them to devils, Psal. cvi. 37? If murder ought to be punished as an injury and dishonour to God, why not also public blasphemy, idolatry, and heresy, obstinately continued in?

4. Magistrates are appointed of God for the *terror* and *punishment of evil doers,* and for the *praise of them that do well,* Rom. xiii. 3, 4. 1 Pet. ii. 14. And are not, Sir, idolaters, blasphemers, profaners of the Sabbath, by teaching of damnable errors or practising of abominable idolatries on it, *evil doers* in God's account, as well as revilers of men, thieves, traitors, murderers, &c.? Are not heresies and idolatries expresly declared by him, *damning works of the flesh,—evil deeds,* Gal. v. 14,—21. 2 Thess. ii. 9,—12. Rev. xiv. 9,—11? Are not heretical teachers declared *evil workers,* Phil. iii. 2. Tit. i. 10, 11.——It must therefore necessarily follow, that magistrates are appointed by God, not to be licensers, protectors, and encouragers, but to be terrors to, and punishers of them, as is *suitable* and *seasonable.*

5. The power, which magistrates have, as *ministers of God for good* to men, ought to be so exercised as most effectually conduceth to make all their subjects live a quiet and peaceable life in all GODLINESS and honesty, and make all men come to the saving knowledge of the truth, 1 Tim. ii. 1, 2, 4. But how, Sir, can their *authoritative* allowing or protecting of men in ungodliness, blasphemy, and idolatry, promote such an end? Hath not God himself testified, that heresies, as well as blasphemy and idolatry, *as a canker*, eat out the doctrine, which is according to godliness, and *increase unto more and more ungodliness*, and make men *worse and worse*, till they be monstrously wicked, 2 Tim. ii. 16, 17. iv. 3, 4. iii. 1,—9, 13. 2 Thess. ii. 3,—12. 1 Tim. iv. 1,—3. vi. 3, 4. 2 Pet. ii. 1,—3, 10,—20. Rom. i. 21,—32. If magistrates protect and encourage obstinate seducers in blaspheming God, reproaching his Son as a mere creature, or as an impostor, or in furiously rending his well compacted body the church, or in corrupting the principles and morals, and ruining the souls of neighbours, children, or servants, how can such as are truly serious and ardently zealous for God, fail to have their righteous souls vexed from day to day, with the damnable doctrines and filthy conversation of these wicked? Psal. cxix. 136, 139, 158. lx x. 9. 2 Pet. ii 8.——To truly zealous saints, a *den of thieves*, is not a more grievous neighbour than a *Synagogue of Satan*.

6. All magistrates ruling over men, must *be just, ruling in the fear of the Lord*, 2 Sam. xxiii. 3. But how can they be *just*, if they dispose of *that protection or encouragement*, to that which dishonours and provokes God to the highest, saps the foundation of all true virtue, and natively produces the most ruinous practices,—*which is due* to that doctrine, worship, and practice, which is *according to godliness*, and promotes glory, honour, immortality, eternal life? How can they rule *in the fear of God*, if, in their magistratical administrations, they shew no regard to that religion, by which his declarative glory is advanced, but instead thereof, license, protect, and encourage, that which infinitely dishonours and offends him?

7. The

7. The fourth commandment, the obligation of which is certainly moral, and *perpetually binding* on magistrates, as well as on heads of families, commands them to cause the weekly Sabbath to be sanctified by all *within their gates*, i. e. all their subjects, Exod. xx. 10. Jer. xvii. 20,---25. And to this the approven example of Nehemiah corresponds, Neh. xiii. 15,--22. Now, if magistrates cannot answer to God, for encouraging or protecting their subjects in their *civil business*, which is of itself lawful and useful,---on the the Sabbath,---how will they account to him, for protecting and encouraging men, in teaching *blasphemous errors*, or practising *abominable idolatries*, on that day ? How can this commandment bind them to restrain what is in itself lawful and useful,--- and yet bind them not to restrain, but *allow, encourage*, and *protect*, that which is in itself infinitely dishonourable to God, their superior, and ruinous to his and their subjects, in both temporal and eternal interests ?------Or, dare you pretend, that the observance of the weekly Sabbath depends one whit less on Revelation, than the doctrine of the Trinity of persons in the Godhead doth.

8. If magistrates have power, on proper occasions, to appoint *religious fasts*, as means of turning away God's wrath, and of procuring or obtaining his blessings to their commonwealth, as it is certain yourself, and perhaps every advocate for *authoritative toleration*, acknowledge, Jonah iii. 6,---10. 1 Sam. vii. 9, 6. 2 Chron. xx. 3,--15 Ezra viii. 21,---23. Neh. ix. 1. Jer. xxxvi. 6, 22, they cannot but have power to establish that religion, and *only that religion* which answers to those ends, and to restrain that damnable heresy, blasphemy, and idolatry, which provoke God's wrath against his subjects. To command their subjects to mourn over the grounds of his anger and supplicate his favour, while at the same time they encouraged and protected them in gross heresy, public blasphemy and idolatry, than which nothing can more provoke his indignation, would be fearful dissimulation with the Most High. Psalm lxvi. 18. Ezek. xiv. 3,---8, If magistrates have power to appoint a Christian fast, and to punish the public contemners

of it, or of their authority, in appointing it,---How can they but have power to eſtabliſh the true Chriſtian religion, and to puniſh, *if ſeaſonable*, the public and inſolent contemners and corrupters of it, and deſpiſers of their authority in eſtabliſhing it?——Dare you pretend, that the upright profeſſion and practice of the Chriſtian religion is leſs calculated to promote the happineſs of a nation in ſubordination to the honour of God, than an occaſional faſt? Or, that a Chriſtian faſt can be obſerved without entering into the very marrow of the doctrines of Revelation?---or that magiſtrates ought merely to require the day to be obſerved in faſting, leaving the manner and object of the worſhip, wholly to the choice of their ſubjects,--recommending the worſhip of devils, as much as that of Jehovah; and ſuppoſing the one as able and ready to avert calamities, and beſtow neceſſary bleſſings, as the other. If you pretend, that God rewarded Ahab or the Ninevites for worſhipping their idols, you muſt prove that God is ſo far from being highly diſpleaſed with idolatry, as himſelf often declares, Deut. xxxii. 16, 17, 21,---26. Judges ii. 14. 2 Kings xvii. 10,---18. Pſalm cvi. 19,---40 Jer. xlviii. 7, 35, l. 38, *&c.*---that he is ready to accept and reward the worſhip of idols, devils, bulls, dogs, cats, ſaints, leeks, onions, conſecrated wafers, *&c.* if men be ſincere in it. Rare doctrine this, for a Preſbyterian clergyman, of this *enlightened age!*

9. If every parent or maſter ought for the welfare of his family, in ſubordination to the honour of the God of all families, to eſtabliſh the true religion in it, Gen. xviii. 19. Joſh. xxiv. 15. to remove idols out of it, Gen. xxxv. 2,—4. and to refuſe ſeducing heretics a lodging in it, 2 John x. 11.——And if according to this injunction, and thoſe approved examples, he ought to extrude a ſeducer, who had entered; or even a member of the family, who obſtinately endeavoured to corrupt the reſt, with damnable error, blaſphemy, or idolatry,---in order to prevent the infection of the family, and hinder the deſtructive wrath of God from falling on them;——Why muſt not magiſtrates, who are *God's miniſters for good*, be allowed power

power and authority to eſtabliſh and promote the true Chriſtian religion, in their *large political families,* and to repreſs or exclude notorious murderers of ſouls, and kindlers of the wrath of God? The relation of a parent or maſter is *no more ſpiritual,* than that of a magiſtrate, makes no man either member or officer of Chriſt's myſtical body, any more than magiſtracy doth.---And I dare defy all the Tolerants on earth, to point out one thing relative to religion, competent to maſters and parents, as ſuch, but magiſtrates may do what is ſimilar; or to prove that the true knowledge, faith, profeſſion and practice of revealed religion, is one whit leſs neceſſary and uſeful in commonwealths, than in families.

10. If the power of eccleſiaſtical rulers extends to all the *civil tranſactions* of *church-members,*---all the *magiſtratical* and *military managements* of kings or emperors not excepted, in ſo far as they are regulated by the law of Chriſt, and are immediately connected with his honour and the good of his church,---there is equal reaſon, that the power of magiſtrates ſhould extend to religious matters, in ſo far as they are connected with the welfare of the ſtate, in ſubordination to the honour of God, as King of nations. No reaſon can be aſſigned, why the vicegerents of God ſhould, as ſuch, act as atheiſts, regardleſs of religion, any more than the meſſengers of Chriſt. Nor, till it be proven, that God, the King of nations, is more inclined to damnable hereſy, blaſphemy, and idolatry, than Chriſt the Head of the church, can it be poſſible to prove, that magiſtrates have one whit more power, *authoritatively* to licenſe, encourage, or promiſe them protection, than church-rulers have;---though as the church is a *ſelect holy ſociety,* called out of the world which lieth in wickedneſs, founded on, and having all her adult members inſtructed by the revelation of Chriſt, the ſame degree of forbearance to cenſure, in the church, as to puniſh in the ſtate, is by no means proper.

11. Unleſs true and falſe religion be equally calculated to render men *good ſubjects, or magiſtrates,* and to promote the peace and proſperity of commonwealths, in ſubordination to the honour of God, as

King of nations, they can never deserve or lawfully enjoy equal encouragement, protection or liberty ---- But the true religion *exalteth a nation*, Prov. xiv. 34 renders it *quiet and prosperous*, 2 Chron. xiv. 1,---7. it teacheth men to *deny ungodliness and worldly lusts, and to live soberly, righteously and godly*, Tit. ii. 11, 12. The fruits produced by it, are *love, joy, peace, long-suffering, gentleness, goodness, faith, meekness, temperance, against which there is no law*, Gal. v. 22, 23.---- whereas, gross heresy, blasphemy and idolatry, debauch mens conscience, make it *seared with a hot iron*, 1 Tim. iv. 2. make their *affections vile*, and their mind and sense *reprobate*, Rom. i. 26, 28. they render men, filled with all deceivableness of unrighteousness,--believers and speakers of lies in hypocrisy, giving 'heed to the damnable doctrines of devils,---proud, doting about questions and strifes of words, whereof cometh envy, strife, railing, evil surmisings, perverse disputings of men of corrupt minds, and destitute of the truth, 2 Thess. ii. 10,--12. 1 Tim. iv. 1, 2, 3. vi. 3, 4. They render times perilous, and men covetous, boasters, proud, disobedient to parents, unthankful, unholy, without natural affection, truce-breakers, false accusers, incontinent, fierce despisers, and extirpaters of those that are good, traitors, heady, high-minded, hypocritical, dissemblers, villainous, corrupters of families, haters and resisters of sound doctrine, reprobate concerning the faith, and waxing worse and worse ;—who will not endure sound doctrine, but after their own lusts, heap up to themselves teachers, having itching ears, and turn away their ears from the truth to fables, 2 Tim. iii. 1,--8, 13. iv. 3, 4. They, as a canker, eat out the principles, profession and practice of piety and virtue, and increase unto more ungodliness, 2 Tim. ii. 16, 17. ——They make men self destroyers,--their pernicious ways much followed,--the way of truth reproached, and dispose them through covetousness with feigned words to make damnable merchandise of souls ; they render men horridly unchaste, presumptuous, self-willed, despisers and revilers of magistrates and church rulers, beguilers of unstable souls, exercised in covetous practices, cursed children,--speakers of great swelling

swelling words of vanity, pretenders to liberty, but rea slaves of corruption, 2 Pet. ii. 1,—3, 10,—19.— They render men ungodly turners of the grace of God into lasciviousness,—filthy dreamers, who defile the flesh, despise dominions, and speak evil of dignities,—blasphemers and calumniators of those things which they know not,—who go in the unnatural and maliciously murderous way of Cain, run greedily after the error of Balaam for reward, and perish in the rebellious gainsaying of Kore,——and are luxurious, unprofitable,——raging waves of the sea, foaming out their own shame,——wandering stars, to whom is reserved the blackness of darkness for ever:—— men of ungodly deeds and hard speeches,—murmurers, complainers, walkers after their own lusts, whose mouth speaketh great swelling words, having mens persons in admiration, because of advantage,—sensual and separating mockers, who walk after their ungodly lusts, Jude iv. 8, 10,—13, 15, 16, 10, 19.—— They render persons and societies full of abominations and filthiness of fornication--a mystery of iniquity, and mother of harlots and abominations in the earth,—drunk with the blood of the saints and martyrs of Jesus,—fighters against Him, who is Lord of Lords, and pretendedly conscientious murderers of his ministers and people, Rev. xvii. 3,—6, 14. John xvi. 2. In fine, they introduce unnatural lusts of the flesh, and tend to fill men with all unrighteousness, fornication, wickedness, covetousness, maliciousness, envy, murder, debates, deceit, malignity, and make them whisperers, backbiters, haters of God, despiteful, proud, boasters, inventers of evil things, disobedient to parents, without understanding, covenant breakers, without natural affection, implacable unmerciful,—who, contrary to their own inward convictions, commit the most abominable crimes, and have pleasure in them that do the like, Rom. i, 21,—23.——These, Sir, if God do know and speak truth, are the native fruits of heresy, blasphemy and idolatry,—these the GOOD SUBJECTS, who are infected with them,—if Providence permit them to reduce their principles to practice. How then is it for the safety of nations, or the honour of God, as King of nations, to have them *authoritatively* tolerated *in his name?*

12. Though God never, in scripture, commands that any lesser mistakes in religion, or a simple neglect of religious duties should be punished; yet he commands magistrates, *suitably* and *seasonably*, to punish, even unto death, idolaters, particularly seducers to it, Deut. xiii. 2,—15. xvii. 2,—7. Exod. xxii. 20. blasphemers, Lev. xxiv. 15, 16. insolent profaners of the Sabbath, Num. xv. 30,—36.——Where in all the New Testament, is there a single hint of the repeal of such laws, any more than of those concerning murder, Gen. ix. 6. Numb. xxxv. 30, 31.?—— Where is a single hint, that Christ's incarnation,— his death for sin, and to save men, abolished these laws and procured for magistrates a right and power, in the name of God, to licence, encourage and protect heretics, blasphemers, and idolaters, who openly and obstinately labour to offend God, and destroy and damn men?

13. God, in scripture, frequently approves of magistrates requiring their subjects to worship the true God, in a right manner,—and of their suppressing and punishing idolatry; as Abraham, Gen. xviii. 19. Jacob, Gen. xxxv. 2, 3, 4. the Judges in the land of Uz, Job xxxi. 26,—28. Moses, Exod. xxxii. 20, 27. Joshua, Josh. xxiv. 14, 15. Asa, 2 Chron. xiv. 2,— 5, xv. 13, 16. Jehoshaphat, 2 Chron. xvii, xix Jehoiada, 2 Chron. xxiii, 16,—19. Hezekiah, 2 Kings xviii. 4, 5. 2 Chron. xxix,—xxxi. Manasseh, 2 Chron. xxxiii. 15, 16. Josiah, 2 Chron. xxxiv. xxxv. 2 Kings xxii, xxiii. Nehemiah, chap. xiii. Jehu, 2 Kings x. 24,—30. and marks with infamy magistrates allowing of their subjects to worship the true God in the high places, 1 Kings xv. 14. xxii. 43. 2 Kings xii. 3 xiv. 4. xv. 4, 35. 2 Chron. xxxiii. 17. The scripture never hints, that those magistrates acted as church officers or merely typical persons, in their reformation work. Nay,

14. Even Heathen magistrates, whom you cannot pretend to have been *ecclesiastical rulers*, have, with his approbation, made laws to promote the honour of

the true God, and against the contemners of him; as Artaxerxes king of Persia, Ezra vii. 13,—26. which *God in mercy put into his heart*, v. 27. Cyrus and Darius Persians, Ezra i. 1,—5 vi. 1,—14. Nebuchadnezzar the Chaldean, Dan. iii. 28, 29. and Darius the Mede, Dan. vi. 26.

15. God promised it, as a blessing to the gospel-church, that magistrates should exercise their power in favours of her revealed religion, and in opposition to false teachers, and their abominable delusions, Isa xlix. 23. " Kings shall be thy nursing fathers, " and queens thy nursing mothers." Isa. lx. 3, 10. 16. " Kings shall come to the brightness of thy ris- " ing,—Kings shall minister unto thee,—Thou shalt " suck the breast of kings." Psalm lxxii. 10, 11. " Kings shall bring presents—shall offer gifts;—all " kings shall fall down before him; all nations shall " serve him." Psalm ii. 8, 10,—12. " I will give " thee, *O Christ*, the heathen for thine inheritance. " ——Be wise now therefore, ye kings, be instruc- " ted ye judges of the earth; serve the Lord with " fear.—Kiss ye the Son," manifesting your cordial subjection to him. Zech. xiii. 2, 3. " I will cut off " the names of idols out of the land, and I will cause " the prophets and the unclean spirit to go out of the " land.—When any shall yet prophesy, then his fa- " ther and his mother shall say unto him, thou shalt " not live, for thou speakest lies in the name of the " Lord, and—shall thrust him through when he pro- " phesieth." Rev. xvii. 16. " The ten horns shall " hate the Whore, and eat her flesh, and burn her " with fire." Rev. xxi. 24. " The kings of the earth " shall bring their glory and honour *unto the gospel " church*." Rev. xi. 15. " The kingdoms of this " world are become the kingdoms of our Lord and " of his Christ."

16 Even the law of nature plainly requires, That magistrates maintain and promote the honour of that God, who gave them all their power and authority, —that God, who is the original and supreme proprietor and Sovereign of nations and societies, and the all-sufficient source of all their happiness;——that they govern their subjects, not as if they were dogs

or swine, having nothing but their bodies to care for, but as men endowed with rational and immortal souls;—that as righteousness exalteth a nation, and sin is the reproach of any people, they should exercise their whole power and authority, as is best calculated to make all their subjects behave most agreeably to the law, and declarative glory of God, and most usefully to each other.——It plainly teacheth, That if God graciously grant us a *supernatural revelation*, directive of our faith, profession and practice, we ought thankfully to receive, believe, profess and obey it;—that, if magistrates ought to restrain and punish gross immoralities, they ought to restrain that error or worship, which, being a manifestly damning work of the flesh, natively leads men into such immoralities;— and that, if heresy, blasphemy and idolatry hinder the progress of virtue, or the increase of good men, who are the principal support and blessings of a society, Isa. vi. 13. lxv. 8. Gen. xviii. 26, 28, 29, 30, 31, 32. they ought to be restrained.——If heresy, blasphemy and idolatry established or authoritatively tolerated, eminently and notoriously provoke God to punish nations with sword, famine, pestilence, poverty, decay of trade, desolation, captivity, or the like, as they have often done even among Heathens, Common sense requires, That every magistrate, from regard to the welfare of his subjects, ought to restrain them, as far as his circumstances can prudently permit,—instead of giving them as much liberty, encouragement or protection as he gives to the religion of Jesus Christ, which hath the promises of this life, and of that which is to come, 1 Tim. iv. 8, Titus iii. 8, 14. Proverbs xiv. 34.

17. If, Sir, as you pretend, magistrates ought to tolerate heresy, idolatry and blasphemy,—then, a power and office derived from God ought to be employed and executed in encouraging the most shocking dishonours and outrage against him;—the authority of God, placed in, and exercised by, magistrates, ought to be set in opposition to his own *immediate* authority, manifested in his word;-- they as *ministers of God for good* to men, ought to licence and encourage his enemies to deny, pervert, and revile his truths contained

in his oracles, and confirmed by the blood of his Son, and to introduce the moſt accurſed and damnable errors into their place, in his church,---ought to give the devil and his agents as much countenance and aſſiſtance in driving men to hell, as they give to Jeſus Chriſt and his faithful ſervants in leading them to heaven,---ought to give a company of wizards as much countenance and protection in worſhipping the devil and his angels, as a ſociety of precious ſaints worſhipping the Lord and his Chriſt, in the beauty of holineſs.——In ſhort, *authoritative tolerations* of hereſy, blaſphemy or idolatry are ſolemn proclamations iſſued forth by the deputies of God, in his name, bearing that Satan and his emiſſaries have full liberty granted them to caſt forth their floods of error, and every abomination that proceeds from it, for the diſhonour of God, and the temporal and eternal deſtruction of men. Nor, for ought I know, have they ever neglected to improve their opportunity; as the iſſues of the tolerations granted by Cromwell, K. James VII. and Q. Anne, in part manifeſt.

How abſurd then, after all the amazing deliverances from it, which God hath mercifully beſtowed upon us.——after all that our fathers have ſuffered from it,——after all our public and ſolemn engagements to God, or to men, againſt it, and when the very acceſſion of our Sovereign K. George and his family to the Britiſh throne, and their eſtabliſhment depends on the nation's deteſtation of Popery, and when the tremenduous deſtruction of its votaries draweth nigh, Rev xiv. xvi. and xviii 4,---8.——for our rulers to grant any *authoritative toleration* of a pretended religion, that *tramples on our Bibles*, which God hath inſpired, and requires us to ſearch as the mean of our eternal ſalvation, 2 Tim. iii. 15,---17. 2 Pet. i. 19,- 21. Iſa. viii. 20. John v. 39. Acts xvii. 11. Col. iii. 16. and *blaſphemes* theſe oracles of God as *imperfect, obſcure, deſtitute of any fixed meaning or conſcience-binding authority* till they receive it from the Pope or his councils, and as infinitely dangerous to the temporal, ſpiritual and eternal intereſts of men, if peruſed without a pontifical licence, Dan. vii. 25. xi. 36. 2 Theſſ. ii. 4. 2 Tim. iv. 4.——a religion, which *overthrows the whole mediation of our Redeemer*, confining his mediatorial work to his manhood,---and making saints, angels, crosses, images, &c. mediators of satisfaction, intercession, or saving influence, along with Him, -- and the Pope and his clergy infallible prophets, sin-expiating priests, and kingly dispensers of spiritual privileges, and formers of laws and offices in the church, Dan. ii. 36,---39. vii. 25. Rev. xvii. 14.----- a *blasphemous* religion, which in the most daring manner, reproacheth and misrepresents God Father, Son, and Holy Ghost, and what belongs to him, and ascribes his excellencies and prerogatives to creatures, Dan. vii, 25. xi. 36,---38. 2 Thess. ii. 4. Rev. xiii. 1, 5, 6. xvii. 3.------a religion *wholly given to superstition*, mingling multitudes of heathenish or other human or devilish ceremonies, with every part of its worship, Dan. vii. 25. 2 Tim. iv. 4 with Mat. xxviii. 20. Deut. xii. 32.------a religion *full of abominable idolatries*, giving to multitudes of saints and angels, images, reliques and consecrated wafers, that worship and glory which is due to God alone, Dan. xi. 38, 39. 2 Thess. iv. 4. Rev. ix. 20, 21. xiii. 3, 4 xiv. 9,---11.------a religion pregnant with the *most shocking villanies*, pretended miracles, dispensing with, or commuting the most solemn engagements,--indulgence of equivocation and mental reservation in oaths,- and inculcating breach of faith with heretics, if for the advantage of the Romish church,------and which, by holding multitudes of sins to be venial,--by the sale of pardons and indulgences,-- by prohibiting clergymen and devotees to marry,-- and by licensing of stews, promotes the most *horrible debauchery*. Dan. xi. 36,---39. 2 Thess. ii. 3, 7, 9,---12. 1 Tim. iv. 1,---3. 2 Tim. iii. 1,---6, 8, 13. Rev. ix. 21. xi. 8. xiii 13, 14. xvi. 13, 14. xvii. 2, 3, 5. xviii. 2.------a *bloody* religion, in the propagation and maintenance of which, about sixty millions of mankind, many of them saints, have been murdered, in the most cruel and inhuman forms, Dan. vii. 25. Rev. viii. 13. ix. 11, 21. xi, 2, 7. xiii. 2, 7. xvii. 6. xviii. 24. xvi. 2.------a religion, the cordial and persevering profession and practice of which, God hath declared *inevitably damning*, 1 Thess. ii 3, 9,---12. Rev. ix. 11. xvii. 11. xiv. 9,---11. xix. 20. xx 10.

OBJECT.

of Heresy, Blasphemy, &c. answered

OBJECT. I. " God alone is the Lawgiver and Lord of mens conscience." ANSW. 1. God is the only absolute, supreme and infallible Lawgiver; He alone hath power to constitute any thing a part of religion. But that no more hinders his magistratical vicegerents to make *political* laws in favours of what he hath declared and instituted in religion, than Christ being Head of the church can hinder her subordinate rulers to make ecclesiastical constitutions in favours of the truth, in his name, Psalm lxxxii. 1, 6. Rom. xiii. 1,—6. 1 Pet. ii. 13, 14. 2. Neither magistrates nor ministers can make any law which of themselves, and as their deeds, bind mens conscience. Their authority is not infallibly exercised; it doth not reach to the inward actings of conscience. They cannot oblige conscience to these actings, or take any cognizance of them. They cannot free it from any guilt contracted by them, or reward it if it doth well, or punish or censure it if it doth amiss. Nor are their constitutions, but God's law, the standard by which it shall be judged at the last day.——But they may make laws or constitutions, which, as originating from, subordinated to, and adopted and ratified by the law of God, bind men to obey for conscience sake, Rom xiii. 1,—4. Mat. xviii. 19. 3. God's being the only Lawgiver of men under the Old Testament as much as now, did not hinder Moses, David, Asa, Jehoshaphat, Hezekiah, Josiah, Nehemiah, Nebuchadnezzar the Chaldean, Darius the Mede, Cyrus, Darius, and Artaxerxes, Persians, or the king of Nineveh to make civil laws in favours of the true religion. 4. If God alone be the Lawgiver and Lord of the conscience, it necessarily follows, that magistrates and conscience, who are his deputies, can have no power to warrant, licence or protect, any thing forbidden by his law, 2 Cor. xiii 8, 10.

OBJECT. II. " Every man hath a natural right to judge for himself, what he ought to do or forbear, especially in religion. He is to be fully persuaded in his own mind, and to follow the dictates of his own conscience. Even the law of God is a rule to him, as he understands it in his own conscience. To force any

any man to do any thing contrary to his conscience, is to force him to sin, for whatsoever is not of faith is sin; and to punish him for following the dictates of his conscience is to punish him for doing his duty."
ANSW. [1.] Already you have made mens conscience the supreme governor of their actions, exalting it above The Most High GOD. [2.] Every man hath a natural right derived from God, to *judge all things by the law of God, and hold fast that which is good*, 1 Thess. v. 21. He hath a right to judge by the law of God what is necessary to be professed and practised, in order to the peace of his conscience, and his fellowship with, and receiving of favours from God. But that no more hinders magistrates *politically* to judge what profession and practice are proper for men, as members of such a particular commonwealth,—or what relative to religion is to be connected with civil encouragements or discouragements,—than it hinders church-rulers, ecclesiastically to judge and define what profession or practice is necessary, in order to comfortable fellowship with such a particular church. [3.] Mens conscience is no Lawgiver at all, but a *witness* of their conduct, and a *judge*, which enquires into the meaning of God's law, and directs accordingly,—and which compares their qualities, profession, and practice with the law of God, and if faithful, approves or disapproves accordingly. [4] The law of God, not men's conscience, is their *supreme and only infallible rule*, which binds even conscience itself, Mark xii. 30. 1 John v. 3 and whatever men do contrary to it, is sinful, let their conscience approve it as much as they will, 1 John iii. 4. Lev. v. 17. 18. Acts xxvi. 9, 10. 1 Tim. i. 13,—16. Whatever proceeds not from the persuasion of a good conscience, founded on the word of God, is sin. It is a sin for mens conscience to err in dictating any thing not perfectly agreeable to the law of God ——How absurd to pretend, that this sin can render another sin duty, or a duty sinful in itself! [5] If mens conscience, in itself, or in its directing, persuading or instigating influence be sustained, as the immediate rule of their conduct, without respect to the word of God, then either their conscience must be *infallible* in its dictates,
which

which it certainly is not, in either saints or sinners, in this world, Rom. vii. 14, 23. Prov. xxviii. 26. Jer. xvii 9. Rom. viii. 7, 8. Tit. i. 15. or, if it be *fallible*, God must have established for men a *fallible* and *deceitful rule* of *truth* and *holiness*,—and so be the author of confusion in religion, since different consciences dictate different things in it.——To make mens conscience their rule in religion, would make God the author and commander of wickedness,——by conscience, requiring the transgression of his own law.——It would make him not only acquit from criminality, but approve as duty, the most damnable errors, horrid blasphemies, detestable abominations, and cruel barbarities, if but dictated by the consciences of Heathens, Mahotans, Papists, &c. in their religion.——It would make him the author of mens ruin, if it were procured by a way which seemed right in their own eyes, Prov. xvi. 25.——It would render it absolutely impossible to convince men of the sinfulness of any thing they had done according to the dictates of their conscience, be it ever so contrary to the law of God. It would render it improper for men to repent of or mourn over any blasphemy, murder of saints, or the like, which their deluded conscience had dictated to them, or to ask, receive, or praise God for the pardoning of it, contrary to 1 Tim. i. 13,---16 with Acts xxvi. 9,-11. Gal. i. 13, 14. Phil. iii. 6. It would open a wide gap for mens doing whatever they pleased, without being chargeable by, at least any man, for it —If men should be executed for the most horrid blasphemy, or abominable idolatry, high treason, or any other deed dictated by their conscience, they would die martyrs for righteousness sake.-- And men ought to believe whatever their conscience dictated to them concerning their state, experience or duty, however contrary to the testimony of God, contained in his word,---contrary to Psalm. iii. 22. & xvi 11. xlii 5, 11. Rev. iii. 17.
[6.] To pretend that the law of God, not in itself, but *as understood by mens conscience*, is their rule, is absurd. It, in the Popish manner, represents the law of God as destitute of sense and authority in itself, and as deriving it from a creature. It in the Quakerish manner, makes the *light within* the rule of mens
con-

conduct. It exalts every man to an equality with, or rather superiority above God, having power to give regulating sense and authority to his word, according as an erroneous and defiled conscience pleaseth. It abolisheth every real standard of religion, every man's particular apprehensions of the meaning of God's word being his binding rule. The same word of God becomes the standard of *Calvinism, Popery, Socinianism,* &c. as different men understand it. It saps the foundation of all mutual trust and confidence among men; and opens a wide inlet for all manner of villany and dissimulation. According to it, mens promises, oaths, vows, and covenants,--their sworn and subscribed Creeds, Articles, Confessions, Formulas, &c. bind them, not according to the common meaning of the words,--but according to the meaning which their conscience, however seared, biassed, or deluded, puts upon them. In fine, it plunges men into the depths of Atheism, according to which every man believes and acts what is right in his own eyes. [7] If mens private judgment of their own acts hindered the magistrates supreme *political* judgment, no laws could be made in matters of religion or any thing else; as some would be readily of a different mind, even in the fundamentals of religion and virtue ——While some believed that Christ was not true God or true man, or that idols might be worshipped, others would believe that oaths might be lawfully violated, heretical princes assassinated, or women and goods used in common. [8.] If other mens private judgment be allowed to be their supreme rule and reason of conduct, it will necessarily follow, that magistrates private judgment must be the rule of their conduct; and that they ought to make and execute such laws as they believe in their own heart to be proper, be they as arbitrary and tyrannical as they will. [9] It is not with mens conscience, and its judgment in religion, any more than in matters of common honesty, that magistratical authority intermeddles, but with their external words and deeds. It only restrains and punisheth such of those as are *manifestly contrary to the laws of God and the land, and as they are hurtful to the com-*
mon-

monwealth, and *the public honour of God as King of nations*. [10.] If all proper means of conviction be used with men who obstinately persist in gross heresy, blasphemy, and idolatry without effect; their mistake doth not arise from a conscience regulating duty, but from one stiffened against duty. And it is perhaps sometimes as difficult to convince a hardened thief, robber, or adulterer of his mistake, as it is to convince a hardened heretic. Men are punishable, not for what their conscience, as the deputy of God, dictates, but for what they would not have done, if they had any proper conscience of duty. [11.] If men slothfully and especially wilfully refuse to use the means of enlightening their conscience by the word of God, they but add to their crimes both before God and men, by pretending conscience. [12.] Mens conscience being as much a director in their conduct towards men, as in their conduct towards God, its influence must have as much force to keep them from accountableness to men, for their theft, murder, calumny, as for their gross heresy, blasphemy and idolatry.

OBJECT. III. " To allow magistrates such power of judging, and of making and executing laws about religious matters, is to render Christians the *servants of men*, contrary to 1 Cor. vii. 23." ANSW. (1,) If so, Christ himself rendered his redeemed favourites *servants of men* under the Old Testament. (2) If so, church rulers being men, as well as magistrates, their restraints and censures, appointed by Christ himself, must as much render Christians *servants of men*.—— Nay to comply with the religious orders of families, would make them *servants of men*. (3.) Servilely to comply with the vain fancies, humours, sinful lusts or laws of men, particularly in religion, is to be the *servants* of men in the sense of this text: but to comply with scriptural restraints, censures, or punishments of wickedness, is to act as *servants of Christ*, and his Father and Spirit.

OBJECT. IV. " To restrain men from what they think right in religion, and especially to punish them for it, is contrary to that Christian charity, which *suffereth long, and is kind,—envieth not,—thinketh no evil, beareth all things, believeth all things, and hopeth all things*, 1 Cor. xlii. 4,—7. contrary to that meekness, mercy and peaceableness exemplified in Christ, and required in Christians, Rom. xv. 1. Gal. vi. 1, 2. Eph. iv 32. 2 Tim. ii. 15. James iii. 15." ANSW. Christian charity rejoiceth *not in iniquity*, but rejoiceth *in the truth*. It requires that nothing should be done out of malice or envy, or rashly on bare surmises, or without due examination of facts and circumstances, but not that rulers, either of church or state, should overlook every scandal or crime contrary to the law of God. Even the undue delay of censure or punishment encourageth men in wickedness, much more would the total overlooking of it, Eccl. viii 11. (2.) The texts quoted in the objection, are directed to Christians and church-rulers. Is therefore all their holy zeal and activity in restraining and censuring the corrupters of the church, according to Christ's command, Rev. ii Rom. xvi. 17. Gal. v. 10. Tit. iii 10. 1 Tim i 20 —contrary to Christian charity, meekness, or mercifulness? Had Moses quite abandoned his unparalelled meekness, when he so zealously punished the Hebrew idolaters, Num. xxxii 3. with Exod. xxxii. 26,—29? Was Jesus Christ destitute of all meekness and mercy, when he appointed the restraints and penalties under the old Testament; and at least the tremenduous censure of excommunication under the new? Was he destitute of all charity, meekness and mercy, in never giving us a hint that these laws are now repealed, as having been cruel and tyrannical? Was he destitute of all charity, meekness and mercy, when the zeal of his Father's house did eat him up,—when he repeatedly drove the buyers and sellers from the temple, John ii. 13,—19. Mat. xxi. 12.

OBJECT. V. "Even under the law, Moses tolerated mens divorcing of their wives for slight causes: Much more doth the gospel dispensation call for liberty to men." ANSW. It is blasphemous to pretend, that the gospel-dispensation allows any more liberty to sin, than the legal did. Must the grace of God be turned into lasciviousness? Jude, ver. 4. Gal. v. 13. (2.) To prevent worse consequences, Moses directed a deliberate and solemn manner of divorce, which tended to render divorces less frequent or irregular, but never warranted divorce for slight causes. (3.) Perhaps

haps you cannot prove, that the perpetual continuance of marriage relation flows as necessarily from the nature of God, as gross heresy, blasphemy, and idolatry are contrary to it; God therefore might sovereignly dispense with the one, though not with the other. (4.) This objection is rather calculated to prove that magistrates should license or tolerate murder, adultery, theft, and other sins against the second table of the moral law, than that they should tolerate heresy, blasphemy, and idolatry, which pertain to the first table.

OBJECT. VI. " Gamaliel's counsel, " Refrain " from these men, and let them alone ; for if this " work be of men it will come to nought, but if it " be of God ye cannot overthrow it," was certainly prudent ; and Gallio's conduct, who cared for no disputes relative to religion, Acts v. 38, 39. & xviii. 15, 17." ANSW. (1.) Prove that Gamaliel's speech was inspired as a rule to us, in all religious disputes, or that magistrates or others ought to be mere sceptics in religion. (2.) That which Gamaliel pled to be let alone, was evidently good, calculated to promote the welfare of both church and state ; and so ought to have had the utmost encouragement from him and his fellow rulers. (3.) Prove, if you can, that the Holy Ghost approves Gallio's carelessness ; or that magistrates like him ought to allow parties at the bar to beat one another.

OBJECT VII " Under the gospel it is promised, That men should beat their swords into plow-shares, and their spears into pruning hooks ; and that there should be none to hurt or destroy in God's holy mountain, Isa. ii. 4. Micah iv. 3." ANSW. (1.) These texts import, that quarrelsome dispositions, and injurious slaughter of men should be remarkably restrained, by the gospel ; but not that magistrates should no more *bear the sword*, or be *terrors* to, and *punishers* of evil doers, Rom. xiii. 1,- 6. 1 Pet. ii. 13, 14 ;--they no more import, that magistrates should not restrain or *seasonably* or *suitably* punish blasphemy and idolatry, than that they should not restrain theft or murder. (2.) The restraint or punishment we plead for, being God's institution, cannot hurt, but profit men,

F 2 mak-

making many fear, and avoid such horrible wickedness. Deut. xvii. 15; nay, sometimes do much good to the restrained and punished persons, Zech. xiii. 6. (3.) If heretics, blasphemers and idolaters be as mischievous persons, as above described from the oracles of God, the restraint of them is a necessary mean to secure the peace of nations and churches. If such scorners be cast out, contention, strife and reproach are repressed, Prov. xxii. 10.

OBJECT. VIII. "Our Saviour commands his servants to let the *tares* grow with the wheat, Mat. xiii. 29, 30." ANSW. He rather represents, that till the last judgment the righteous should never be fully separated from the wicked. (2.) If it were a command, it is given to church rulers rather than to magistrates, and so might, with more apparent propriety, be pled in favours of ecclesiastical toleration, of heretics, idolaters, blasphemers. (3) If these *tares* mean only hypocrites, who have a visible appearance of holiness or innocency, we plead, that neither magistrates nor ministers ought to attempt plucking them up. If they mean all the *children of the devil*, as ver. 38. your objection ought honestly to plead, that no crimes of theft, murder, &c. manifesting them to be such, ought to be restrained or punished.

OBJECT. IX. "By rebuking his disciples, who would have commanded fire from heaven to consume those Samaritans who refused him lodging in his way to Jerusalem; and by his declaring, *That he came not to destroy mens lives, but to save* them, Luke ix. 51,---56. our benevolent Saviour plainly intimated, That under the gospel, magistrates ought to lay no restraint on heresy, blasphemy or idolatry." ANSW. (1.) As these Samaritans did not live under magistrates or laws, which established the true religion, it is not pled, that even their gross heresy, blasphemy, or idolatry, however notorious and obstinate, could have been regularly punishable by men. (2) They were in this matter guilty of no heresy, blasphemy or idolatry,---or of attempting to seduce or disturb Christ or his disciples,---but merely of not giving lodging to a mean-like Jew, of whose Messiahship they had but little, if any information or proof. (3.) Though the Samaritans

tans had been guilty of gross heresy, blasphemy and idolatry, publicly and obstinately professed and practised, contrary to the civil laws of the country, and been regularly punishable,—Christ's disciples being no magistrates in that place, had no right to call them to account. (4.) The disciples never sought to have the contempt shown to themselves and their Master punished by the civil law, but by the *miraculous vengeance of God*. Without any warrant from God, and to gratify their own proud, passionate, and revengeful temper, they would have required him to work a miracle for the destruction of these poor ignorant Samaritans.——So, if you will drag in this text, it ought to be to prove, That neither God nor ministers ought to restrain heretics, blasphemers, or idolaters. (5.) While Christ was in his debased state, obeying and suffering for the salvation of mankind, it would have been extremely improper for God, visibly to punish every slight put upon him. But his coming to *save men* with an everlasting salvation, can no more infer, that he came to protect criminals from just punishment by men, than that he came to save obstinate unbelievers from hell. He came to *save mens lives*, by saving them from their sins, not by protecting and warranting them in a public and obstinate commission of them. There is no hint in scripture, that he, who was manifested to destroy the works of the devil, came to procure men a liberty of conscience, or a magistratical licence or protection in public and gross heresy, blasphemy, and idolatry, more than in theft, murder, adultery. It would be highly blasphemous to suppose it.

OBJECT. X. " Christ requires us not to judge others,—to judge nothing before the time. Mat. vii. 1. 1 Cor. iv. 5. We ought to believe our own opinions in religion to be as probably erroneous, as those of our opponents; and if they do not acknowledge themselves heretics, blasphemers, or idolaters, we ought never to hold them such, or plead for their being restrained as such." ANSW. (1.) We must never rashly or uncharitably judge others, or judge their hearts and intentions, which God alone knoweth. But that will no more infer, that magistrates ought to give no judgment

ment about religious matters, than that magistrates and ministers should judge of nothing at all respecting either God or men, but encourage every person to live as his inclinations direct him. (2.) Is there indeed no certainty in religion? If men ought to be *complete Sceptics* in it; why not as well *downright atheists*? (3.) If mens own acknowlegments be sustained as the standard of our judgment concerning them, what rare work must ensue! None ought to be held blasphemers, heretics, or idolaters, till they have become penitent convicts. None ought to be held thieves murderers, calumniators, &c. till they acknowledge themselves such. All impenitent criminals must thus escape every degree of infamy, restraint or punishment.

OBJECT. XI. "Men ought to be *persuaded*, not *forced* into faith and holiness. It is in vain to attempt rooting out corruptions, especially in religion, out of mens outward behaviour unless they be first rooted out of their hearts." ANSW. (1.) It requires no small share of *ignorance*, *impudence* and *fraud*, to insinuate that the many thousands of Protestant advocates for the magistrates power to restrain gross heresy, blasphemy or idolatry, plead for the FORCING of men to faith and holiness, when they so harmoniously plead for the contrary. (2) None ought to be forced into the faith and profession of the true religion, as hath been repeatedly declared, but all proper methods taken to render their compliance judicious and voluntary. Yet that will not infer, that no man ought to be restrained from, or even *suitably* and *seasonably* punished for, open and gross heresy, blasphemy or idolatry, which, while they publicly oppose, insult, and undermine the true religion,—produce terrible immoralities and disorders in churches and nations, and draw upon them the ruinous vengeance of God;—and far less will it infer, that magistrates, as vicegerents of God, ought, in his name and authority, to *license* a false religion, and promise men protection and encouragement in it No magistrate hath power to force me to esteem, love, delight in, sympathize with, maintain, or even commend my neighbour. But he hath power to refuse me a warrant to calumniate, rob or murder him, and even to reſtrain or puniſh me for ſo doing. It would be abſurd to attempt forcing of the Britiſh Jacobites, to believe and ſolemnly profeſs, that K. George, not the Pretender is rightful Sovereign of this kingdom. But would it therefore be abſurd, to reſtrain and puniſh them for publicly and inſolently reviling him as an uſurper,—or ſeducing their fellow ſubjects to dethrone him,—or for taking arms againſt him, or paying his juſt revenues to the Pretender? (3) It is certain, that Chriſt, who hath power over the hearts of all men, curbed the external corruptions of the Jewiſh buyers and ſellers in the temple, without firſt caſting the corruptions out of their heart. And pray would you have all thieves, robbers, murderers, &c. to have full liberty in their courſes, till their wickedneſs can be got rooted out of their heart?

Object. XII. "Such is the reaſonableneſs and the glory of divine truths, that if they be but freely, clearly and diſtinctly preached, their native luſtre will render them victorious over every error and corruption in religion, however boldly publiſhed, or craftily varniſhed. What a ſingular advantage hath it been to Britain, that Deiſts have had full freedom to make their attacks upon the Chriſtian religion, and ſo to occaſion ſo many glorious defences of it?" Answ. (1.) Did not God under the Old Teſtament, know the conquering power of his truth as well as you do? Did not Chriſt know it when he drove the buyers and ſellers from the temple. (2) Did the inexpreſſibly amiable and edifying conduct of Jeſus Chriſt, the way, the truth and the life, render him the univerſal, the fixed DARLING of the Jewiſh nation, among whom he went about doing good? You dare not pretend it. And yet it is certain that examples do more affect than inſtructions. (3) You muſt not only, with Pelagians, deny original ſin, but effectually diſprove it, before your objection can have any ſenſe in it.—While men are ſo blinded by Satan and their own luſts, and ſo full of enmity againſt God, they cannot but be much more diſpoſed to receive and practiſe error, than to diſcern, embrace, and practiſe goſpel-truths, however clearly and faithfully preached, 1 Cor. ii 14. Rom. viii. 7, 8. 2 Cor. iv. 3, 4. Iſa. liii. 1. vi. 9, 10. (4) The

The common experience of every one, who attempts to instruct children and servants in the truths of God, even when they are young, and their minds most unbiassed, irrefragably demonstrates, that almost any thing is more readily embraced than the plain truths of the gospel; and that earnest prayers, serious admonitions, external encouragements, and Christian nurture, have all enough, and too often more than enough of work, to make men learn them. (5.) If professed Christians, by encouraging others in gross error and wickedness, provoke God to give up themselves to strong delusions, that they may believe lies, will the native lustre of divine truths then enlighten and captivate them? Far,—very far from it, 2 Thess. ii. 10, —12. 2 Tim. iii. 13. iv. 3, 4. (6.) If we do evil in licensing, encouraging, or protecting the free propagation of gross errors, that good reputation may be thereby occasioned, our damnation is just, Romans iii. 8. (7.) Few of those boasted *glorious defenders of Christianity* are real and thorough friends to the gospel of Christ, but often proceed upon the Arminian, and sometimes the Socinian scheme, the last of which is as bad, if not worse, than Heathenism itself.——And, it is certain, that TENS, if not HUNDREDS, have been seduced by deistical publications, for every ONE, that has been been converted from Deism by almost all these defences of the Christian religion.

OBJECT. XIII. "Christ hath appointed for his church, rulers of her own, who govern her in every duty of religion." ANSW. (1.) This can no more prove, that magistrates ought to make and execute no laws respecting the duties required by the first table of the moral law, than it will prove that they ought to make no laws respecting duties of the second table,—since church-rulers are as much authorized by God to govern, in the one as in the other. Let magistrates and church-rulers be allowed to govern their distinct departments in their different manner, in the very same things, and nothing but harmony, order and advantage will ensue. (2.) Magistrates as well as church rulers, are divinely denominated, *Rulers, Watchmen, Shepherds*,—and therefore ought *politically* to direct, govern and feed their subjects as members of the commonwealth, by making and executing wholsome laws relative to both tables of God's law;—while ministers *ecclesiastically* feed them, as *members of the visible church*, by preaching the gospel, administring the sacraments, and exercising church government and discipline, 1 Tim. ii. 1, 2, 4. Rom. xii. 1,—6. 2 Chron. xiii. 10, 11. & xvii. xix. Neh. xiii. 10,—17. Ezek. xxxiv. 9, 10.

OBJECT. XIV. "The church hath *sufficient* power in herself to obtain every end necessary to her own welfare. That cannot be an ordinance of Jesus Christ, which needs any *foreign* assistance to gain its proper end." ANSW. (1.) The church hath as sufficient power to gain her ends, with respect to the duties of the second table, as to gain her ends in what respects the first table. Will it therefore follow, that magistrates ought to make no laws respecting murder, unchastity, theft, calumny, &c? (2.) Public transgressions of the first table of the moral law injure *the state*, as well as they do the church. The state, which also hath a power in itself sufficient to gain all its ends, necessary to promote its own welfare, ought therefore to restrain or punish such transgressions *as crimes* injurious to itself, while the church restrains and censures them as *scandals* defiling and hurtful to herself. (3.) If soundness in the faith, purity in worship, holiness in practice, and beautiful order in the church, be an excellent mean of promoting the happiness of that nation, where the church hath her residence, magistrates ought to promote those things, out of a regard to the prosperity of their state, in subordination to the honour of God. (4.) However complete the intrinsic power of the church be, it is manifest, that it can be exercised to more advantage, if parents, masters, and magistrates regularly exert their power in promoting the true religion, in their different departments.—It is no less certain, that after the church hath done her utmost, by conference, injunction and censure, some turbulent heretics or blasphemers may do as much, if not more, hurt to her than before, unless magistrates restrain or punish them.

OBJECT. XV. "For almost three hundred years after Christ, the truths of the gospel gloriously prevailed against errors and corruptions, without any care of magistrates to restrain or punish the erroneous." ANSW. (1.) It was proper, that the Christian religion should be spread in the world, not only without the countenance of the civil magistrate, but also in opposition to his severe laws and bloody persecutions, that it might the more abundantly appear to be of God. (2.) In that period, it prevailed notwithstanding the most furious opposition, and the cruel persecution and murder of millions of its adherents, as well as without magistratical assistance. Will you therefore plead, that peace and freedom in preaching the gospel ought to be hated and avoided, and furious persecution coveted and prayed for? (3) In that period, the miraculous powers, which attested the doctrines of Christ did more than balance the want of magistratical helpfulness to the truth, Heb. ii. 4.—— (4.) In that period, the hardships to which Christians were exposed, deterred such naughty persons from entering the church, as might have plagued her with their blasphemies and heresies. (5) And nevertheless, even then blasphemers and heretics did no small hurt to the church. (6.) If God had not reckoned the magistratical countenance a real blessing to his church, he had never promised it, as in the texts above quoted.

OBJECT. XVI. "It is horrid cruelty and unchristian persecution to restrain or punish men for believing, teaching, and worshipping, according to the dictates of their own conscience, as charity obligeth us to believe is the case with heretics, blasphemers and idolaters.—It is *altogether diabolical, the very worst part of Popery,* and that which *peculiarly supports the whole Antichristian scheme.*—Men ought to follow the dictates even of an erring conscience." ANSW. (1.) Where is your proof, from either scripture or reason, that an erring conscience binds men to believe, teach or practise, gross heresy, blasphemy or idolatry, any more than their promises or vows to do evil, bind to performance?—or than it can bind them to theft, murder, adultery, calumny, or the like?—If we
have

have an erring conscience, our immediate duty is to get rid of that error, by the illumination of God's word, as being sinful in itself, especially if procured through sloth or wickedness; it will hinder our right performance of duty, but can never make sin lawful. If, Sir, you can believe, that an erring conscience, can outdo the almighty power of God, in making heresy, blasphemy, or idolatry innocent things, you may quickly believe, that a Romish priest can outdo his Maker, in making a God, and then eating him, in the mystery of transubstantiation. (2.) Even when conscience is perfectly clear, pure and unbiassed, it is wholly subordinated and subjected to the authority of God's law.——How can the entrance of sinful error into it, exalt it above his law, and make such a God of it, as can stamp its wicked dictates into incontroulable laws, in opposition to the mandates of Jehovah himself.—This will not only prove, that Adam and Eve became Gods by the entrance of sin, but go far to justify Popes and devils in the whole of their conduct. (3.) If the devil, who deceiveth the world, get into mens conscience by his strong delusions, hath God allotted him that as a quiet city of refuge, from which no means ought to be used to dislodge him, and from which he may use the whole man unrestrained in his service,—in sacrificing children to Moloch, murdering saints, blaspheming God, &c. ? (4.) Where is your proof, that I ought to believe, that the man, who hath access to the Bible, acts according to the dictates of his conscience in gross heresy, blasphemy or idolatry, any more than that he acts according to them, in murder, treason, theft, unchastity, &c. ? Men have laboured and suffered as much, in courses of the latter kind, as in those of the former, and died as impenitently at last. (5) If pretence of conscience, and more than pretence in favours of sin we can never be certain of, be a sufficient ground for magistrates licensing, encouraging and protecting men in contradicting and blaspheming God, or robbing him of his worship, to bestow it on devils,—or in robbing his church of his oracles or ordinances,—in murdering the souls of men, and sowing the seeds of confusion and every evil work,—Why ought it not to warrant their licenſing, encouraging and protecting them in high treaſon, calumny, theft, robbery, murder?—It is hoped, you, who are ſo generous in allowing men, if they can but pretend conſcience for it, to abuſe and rob Jehovah, will be as ready to allow them equal freedom, if they can but pretend conſcience, in abuſing and injuring yourſelf. If God's giving up men to *ſtrong deluſions*, that they may believe lies warrant magiſtrates to encourage or protect them, in ſpreading groſs hereſy, or in open blaſphemy and idolatry, Why ought not his giving them up to *vile affections*,—to their own hearts luſts, equally to warrant their encouraging and protecting of them in open whoredom, beſtiality, inceſt, robbery, *&c.* ? Men can as little conquer their luſts and cleanſe their hearts, as they can rectify the errors of their conſcience. (6.) It is infallibly certain, that God himſelf, under the Old Teſtament appointed magiſtrates to reſtrain and puniſh men for blaſphemy and idolatry, let their conſcience dictate them as ſtrongly as it pleaſed.——Had men in theſe early ages no conſcience to govern them? Or did God then, like the old faſhioned Proteſtants, not underſtand human liberty and the rights of mens conſcience?—Did he indeed then ſo far miſtake his way, as to appoint what is ſo *cruel* and *diabolical;* what is the very *worſt part of Popery*, and the *principal ſupport of that abominable ſyſtem?* Or hath God, or the nature of ſin, cruelty and tyranny, been changed? How ſhocking the thought!

OBJECT. XVII. " As mens natural and civil rights nowiſe depend upon their being orthodox Chriſtians, magiſtrates ought to protect them in theſe privileges, be their opinions and worſhip what they will; nay, to give them legal ſecurity for their protection of them, in theſe opinions and worſhip, that they may not be expoſed to the caprices of particular magiſtrates."

ANSW. [1.] The Chriſtian liberty, which Chriſt purchaſed, is not a liberty to commit ſin, but a ſpiritual freedom from it, Gal. v. 1, 13 Luke i. 74, 75. Heb. xii. 28, 29. Chriſt came not to ſave mens lives from reſtraint or puniſhment required by his own law, in order that they, by ſpreading groſs hereſy, blaſphemy, and idolatry, might ruin nations and damn mens fouls. [2.] You might have forborne to demand *legal* or *authoritative* licenses for men to blaspheme God, worship devils in his stead, &c. till you had proven Satan to be the absolute proprietor and governor of this world, and the primary granter of all civil and natural rights to men ;—or proven, that God, who is infinitely holy, just and good, hath, or can, give men natural or civil rights protecting them in public blasphemy, idolatry, or the like, any more than rights protecting them in incest, robbery, murder ; or that magistrates, as his ministers, ought, in his name and authority, to grant men such rights. [3.] If God hath so frequently turned men out of their civil property and life for their idolatry and blasphemy, Isa. x, xiv, xxxvii, xlvi, xlvii. Jer. xlviii, li. Ezek. xxxv —how absurd to require magistrates, who are *his ministers for good* to men, to execute their office, which is *his ordinance,* Rom, xiii. 1,—6. in encouraging and protecting men, in openly and insolently contradicting, blaspheming, rebelling against, and robbing him ?— Ought the Sheriff and Justices of peace in Britain, as the *king's ministers for good* to the nation, to have executed their office in protecting the arch-rebels in 1715, and 1745, in the undisturbed enjoyment of all their civil rights, or to have given them new legal securities, in order to enable them, more boldly and successfully to carry on their treacherous and murderous rebellion against his Majesty ? Or ought they, by proclamation, to warrant all the subjects in their respective counties to revile, rob, and take arms against our king and parliament, and promise them protection in so doing, but always prohibiting them to injure their fellow subjects ?

OBJECT. XVIII. " Magistrates ought not to rule their subjects by the Bible, but by the civil laws of the nation, according to which they are admitted to their power, by their subjects, from whom all their power originates " ANSW. [1.] That magistrates power originates from their subjects is a notion *plainly atheistical.* It originates in God himself, Rom. xiii. 1, 2. Rom. xi. 36. Psalm lxxv. 7. Dan. ii. 21. [2.] If magistrates must regulate their government by no other
law

law than that which they or their subjects have established for themselves or one another; they must act as atheists independent of God, in the execution of an office wholly derived from him, and for every act of which they must be accountable to him. If the useful laws of one nation, may be adopted into the civil law of another, Why may not the will of God, the supreme governor of nations, declared in his laws of nature and revelation, be also adopted into it? Are God's laws more dishonourable or dangerous,—more unfit to be adopted into our civil law, than those of our sinful neighbours? Is the Scotch law the worse, that many of God's statutes, prescribed in his word, have been adopted into it,—nay, that all the leading doctrines of Christianity contained in our two Confessions of Faith and Catechisms have been adopted into it, and the Confessions themselves expresly ingrossed into acts of Parliament?—Indeed, if nations adopt nothing of the manifested will of God, into their civil law, it will contain nothing but useless trifles. Will these be fit for directing the administrations of *ministers of God for good* to men, or for securing, and promoting the important welfare of any nation under heaven? (3.) If all civil authority to make laws, resident, either in subjects or magistrates, be necessarily derived from God, as *Former* and *King of nations*;— If magistrates be *ordained of God*, to be *ministers of God for good* to men, to be for *terror* and *punishment*, and *revengers of evil doers*, and a *praise of them that do well*, and to *be obeyed* for *conscience sake,—for the Lord's sake*, Rom. xiii. 1,—6. 1 Pet. ii. 13, 14. Common sense loudly demands, That neither their will nor that of their subjects, but the manifested will of God, their independent and infinitely high superior, should be the *supreme rule and standard* of all their administrations; and that no civil law should or can bind either magistrates or their subjects, but in so far as it is agreeable and subordinated to the laws of God.

OBJECT. XIX "Magistracy being an office, not founded in revelation, but in the law of nature, the whole execution of it ought to be regulated by that law of nature, not by the will of God revealed in scripture." ANSW. (1.) I thank you for so quickly over-

overturning your preceding objection, and adopting the *divine law* of nature, instead of *your civil law*, as the supreme standard of magistratical administration. (2.) According to your objection, parents, masters, children and servants, must regulate their performance of relative duties, merely by the law of nature, without taking the smallest assistance from the directions of the Holy Ghost in scripture. No parents or masters must instruct their children or servants in the knowledge of the doctrines, promises, laws, worship, or virtue required in the Bible, as these relations *depend no more on Revelation than magistracy doth*. I defy you to prove they do. In performing the duty of our natural or civil relations, we must act as *mere deists*, ignorant of, or pouring contempt on the inspired oracles of the Great GOD, our Saviour.——What hurt have the laws of revelation done to such relative duties, that they must be thus infamously excluded from being any part of a rule of them? (3) No man can truly obey the law of nature, without heartily embracing and chearfully improving whatever revelations God is pleased to bestow on him,—as such revelations proceed from the same divine authority as the law of nature; and must be a noted means of promoting true and proper obedience to it.—To exclude divine revelation, when granted, from regulating our performance of relative duties, must therefore not only amount to an *heathenish* contempt of the scriptures, but to an *atheistical* contempt of the law of nature, which necessarily requires us to adopt divine Revelation for our supreme rule, whenever it is graciously granted to us.

OBJECT. XX. " Many of the above-mentioned instances of magistrates care about religion, and their restraint and punishment of idolaters, blasphemers, and false prophets, related merely to the Jewish Theocracy which was *typical*, and therefore not now to be copied." ANSW. [1.] Many of the above-mentioned instances, particularly those respecting Heathens, or contained in the promises to the gospel church, have not the least appearance of being typical. Nay, I defy you to prove that the instances of Jewish rulers were *merely* typical. [2.] These typical magistrates of the Jewish

Jewish nation also exercised laws relative to murder, theft, unchastity, treason, and other matters of the second table of the moral law. Ought therefore no magistrates now to do so? The laws respecting duties of the second table pertained as much to the Jewish Theocracy, as those relating to the first. Must therefore the Christian magistrate, for fear of copying the Jewish Theocracy, meddle with no morality at all? [3.] Must every thing that was once typical, be now, under the gospel, excluded from regulating authority? Must all the excellent patterns of Abel, Enoch, Noah, Abraham, Isaac, Jacob, Joseph, Job. Moses, Aaron, Samuel, David, and other Hebrew saints be rejected as typical and useless?——Must all the laws directing to elect men, *fearing God, and hating covetousness,* to be magistrates, or directing them to judge justly, impartially and prudently, and to punish murderers, adulterers, thieves, robbers, &c. be discarded as typical? Must the weekly Sabbath, public fasts and thanksgivings be laid aside as typical,—a mere sign between God and the Israelites? Must the ten commandments, and all the explications of them in the Old Testament be discarded, as published in a typical manner, and to a typical people, and used as the principal part of their rule of government in the Jewish Theocracy? [4] As the Jewish church was a REAL church, and not MERELY TYPICAL, so their State was a REAL commonwealth or kingdom, and not MERELY TYPICAL. Whatever therefore pertained to it, *as a real commonwealth,* is imitable in any other. [5.] The Jewish Church and State were as REALLY DISTINCT, as the Church and State are now; though I do not say precisely in the same manner. (1.) They differed in respect of REGULATING LAWS. The ceremonial law directed the Jewish church. The judicial directed the affairs of their state. (2.) They differed in their respective ACTS. The Jews worshipped God, offered sacrifices, and received sacraments, not as members of that state, but as members of that church. They punished evil doers by fines, imprisonment, banishment, burning, stoning, and hanging; and fought with enemies, &c. not as a church, but

but as a state. (3.) They differed in respect of CON-TROVERSIES. To the church pertained the *matters of the Lord*, and a judging of leprosies, and between statutes and judgments. To the state belonged the *matters of the king*, and to judge between blood and blood, 2 Chron. xix. 10, 11. Deut. xvii. 8. (4.) They differed in respect of OFFICERS. The priests were the only stated officers in the church, and prophets a kind of occasional ones. Elders, Judges and Kings were governors in the State. The priests might not take the civil sword out of the hand of the magistrates; nor the magistrates offer sacrifices, burn incense, or otherwise execute the priest's office. (5.) They differed in respect of CONTINUANCE. When the Jewish civil power was taken away by the Romans, the constitution of their church remained, in the days of our Saviour's debasement. And even now the Jews pretend to be a church, but not to be a state. (6.) They differed in respect of VARIATION. The constitution of their church remained much the same under Moses, Joshua, the Judges, the Kings, and after the captivity. But the form of the state underwent great alterations. (7.) They differed in respect of MEMBERS. Proselytes of the covenant were complete members of the Jewish church; but had not the same dignities or marriages allowed them in the State, as the natural Israelites. Nor had the proselytes of the gate any church privileges, though they had some civil ones. (8.) They were governed by different COURTS. The church had her courts of the Synagogue, and her ecclesiastical Sanhedrin.—The state had her courts of the gate, &c. and her civil Sanhedrin;—though often some Levites were judges in both, as our ruling elders in the church, may, at the same time, be civil judges, Exod. xxiv. 1. Deut. xvii. 8,—12. 1 Chron. xxxiii. 4, & xxvi. 30, 32. 2 Chron. xi. 8, 10, 11. Jer. xxvi. 8,—11, 16. xviii. 18. with Deut xvii. 10, 11, 12. Ezek vii. 26 2 Kings vi. 32. Zech. vii. 1,—3. Psal. cvii. 32. Ezek. xiii. 9. Mat. ii 4. xvi. 21. xxi. 23. xxvi. 57, 59. xxvii. 1, 12. Luke xxii. 66. Acts iv. 5. Some Jewish Rabbins expressly distinguish between their judges and their church elders in the same places. (9.) They

H differed

differed in their CENSURE of offenders. In the church, offenders were suspended from sacred fellowship, by *a casting out of the Synagogue,* or *a cutting off from God's people or congregation.* John ix. 22. & xii. 42. Exod. xii. 15, 19 Num. xix. 13, 20. Lev. xxii. 3. with Gen iv. 14.—Lev. vii. 20, 21. with v. 2, —1 Cor. v. 6, 7. 8, 13. with Exod. xii. 15, 19. Gen. xvii. 14. with Acts iii. 23 Psal i. 5. Gen. xxv. 17. In the state, they were call off by death or outlawry. (10) Profane and scandalous persons were excluded from the Jewish temple-service and passover, while they retained their civil rights in the state, Ezek xliv. 7, 9 Deut. xxiii. 18. Jer. vii. 9,—11. Ezek. xxiii. 38, 39. 2 Chron. xxiii. 19 with 1 Cor. v. 11 Psal. cxviii. 19, 20. & xv. 1,—5. & xxiv. 3, 4. & l. 16,—20. Ezek. xxvi. 22, 26 Ezra x. 8, 16, 17. & vi. 21. *.—
[6.] There was no such difference between the Jewish magistracy, especially after their rejection of the Theocracy, under Samuel, 1 Sam. viii. 5, 7, 19 & x :. 12, 17, 19. and the magistracy in Christian countries, as it is often pretended. (1.) The Jewish magistracy was an *ordinance of God.* Exod xviii. Num. xi. Deut. i. xvii. & xvi. 18, 19. Magistracy is still an ordinance of God, to be submitted to for the Lord's sake, Rom. xiii. 1,—6 1 Pet. ii. 14. (2.) Notwithstanding God's appointment of particular persons to be their kings, the Hebrew nation had the power of electing and admitting them to their office, 1 Sam. x, xi, xvi. 2 Sam. ii. 4. & v. 3. 1 Chron. xii. Our magistrates are *powers ordained of God,* Rom. xiii. 1,—6. and yet an *ordinance of men,* 1 Pet. ii. 13. (3) God himself was the supreme governour of the Hebrew nation, Deut. xii 32. Hos. xiii. 10. God is still *King of nations, Most High, King of the whole earth,* Jer. x 7. Psalm lxxxiii. 18. xlvii. 7. (4.) The Israelites were God's peculiar kingdom, 1 Sam. xii. 12. Hos xiii, 10. Nations which generally profess the Christian religion, are the *kingdoms of our Lord and of his Christ,* Rev. xi. 15. (5) The Jewish magistrates were deputies and vicegerents of God the sovereign King, 1 Chronicles

---

* See Gillespy's *Aaron's Rod blossoming,* Part I. Leusden's *Philologus Hebræo mixtus,* P. 338, 339.

xxix. 23. 2 Chron. ix. 6, 7. Psal. lxxxii. 1, 6. Magistrates are still *powers ordained of God, ministers of God for good*, to whom we must be subject for conscience sake,—for the Lord's sake, Rom. xiii. 1,—6. 1 Pet. ii. 13. By Christ kings still reign, and princes decree justice, even all the judges of the earth, Prov. viii. 15, 16. with Eph. i. 22. (6.) The manifested will of God was the proper statute book of the Jewish civil law, Deut. xvii. The will of God manifested in the laws of nature and revelation, are the supreme standard of all civil laws in the world, in which every human constitution ought to be founded, and by which the whole binding force of it is circumscribed, Acts iv. 19. & v. 29. Psal. ii. 10,—12. and hence human laws become an *ordinance of God*, Rom. xiii. 2. (7.) The judicial laws of the Hebrew nation, regulated that which pertained to their kings, judges, warriors, fields, houses, injuries, crimes, punishments, mortgages, marriages, *&c*. Exod. xxi,—xxiii. Deut. xviii, xx, Lev. xviii, xx. Num. xxxvi,—xxxviii, *&c*. Our civil laws regulate the same things. (8) Among the Jews, notorious disobedience to the declared will of God was held rebellion against him, the King of the nation, and to be condignly punished, as it tended to the good of the state, Hob. ii. 2. & x. 28. Notorious disobedience to the manifested will of God ought to be still held as rebellion against Him, as king of nations, and to be condignly punished, as tends to the welfare of the state,—magistrates being still set up by God to be *terrors, revengers*, and *punishers of evil doers*, and bound *not to bear the sword in vain*, Rom. xiii. 1,—5. 1 Pet. ii. 13, 14. Nor hath it been yet proven, That our magistrates, who have the scriptures, ought to pay less real regard to them in the stating of crimes, than the Jewish rulers did. (9) The Jewish magistrates were appointed to promote the welfare of the church, in order to promote the welfare of the state, in subordination to the honour of God, the King of the nation. Magistrates are still bound to do the same, as they have opportunity, Isa. xlix. 23. & lx. 3, 10, 16 Rev. xvii. 16. & xxi. 24, 26. Rom. xiii. 1,—6. 1 Pet. ii. 13, 14. 1 Tim. ii. 1,—4. (10.) The Jewish church and state, as hath been just

now

now proven, were really distinct from, and independent of each other, having different laws, officers, courts, privileges, penalties, &c. The christian church and the civil state of Christians are no less distinct and independant of each other. (11.) Nevertheless, the purity of the Jewish church, contributed much to the welfare of their state, and the right management of their state to the prosperity of their church; and bad management in the one always tended to the hurt of the other, Deut. xxviii,——xxxii Lev. xxvi. Judges i, ——xiii. 1 Sam. ii.——to 2 Chron. xxxvi. Isa. i —— to Mal. iv. Isa i. 19, 20. & iii. 10, 11. And still righteousness exalteth a nation, and sin is the reproach and ruin of any people, Prov. xiv. 34. (12.) God never commanded the Jewish magistrates to *force* their true religion upon their Heathen neighbours, Philistines, Moabites, Ammonites, or Syrians, whom they conquered, or to put them to death for their idolatry. Nor hath He ever commanded magistrates, who have embraced the true Christian religion to FORCE men by fire or sword, or any like punishments, to embrace and profess it,—or to inflict the same punishments upon blasphemers or idolaters in unenlightened countries, which they may do upon such as obstinately rebel against and apostatize from the truth, amidst plentiful means of conviction and establishment in it. (13) Never did God, that I know of, require the Jewish magistrates to punish any of their subjects for *lesser faults*, however open or manifest, or to punish them for the *simple neglect* of duties *strictly religious*,—or to annex sentences of outlawry and of death to ecclesiastical *cutting off* by excommunication from the church. Nor can I find, that he hath enjoined any such thing upon the Christian magistrate. (14) Among the Jews, some things partaking of both a civil and religious nature, did, in these different respects, fall under the government of both Church and State. Even circumcision itself was a national badge as well as a religious seal of God's covenant.——Among Christians, public fasts and thanksgivings, calling of Synods, &c. do, in different respects, fall under the power of both church and state.——Pretend therefore no more, that there is a *total difference* between the case of our magistrates

gistrates, and that of the Jewish, recorded in scripture.

OBJECT. XXI. "To allow magistrates a power of judging, making and executing laws, about religion, and of punishing men for erroneous opinions, or for disturbing the peace and order of the church, as in our Confession of Faith and Second Book of Discipline, altogether confounds the kingdoms of Christ with the kingdoms of this world, contrary to John xviii. 36." ANSW. Sir, Have you in an honest and orderly manner, renounced these Confessions of Faith, as plainly and publicly as you solemnly avowed, if not also, subscribed a stedfast adherence to the Westminster one, at your ordination? Dare you, one day, call God, angels and men to witness, that you sincerely avow that Confession of Faith to be the Confession of your Faith, and that you sincerely believe the WHOLE DOCTRINE contained in it, to be founded on the word of God, and will constantly adhere to and maintain the same all the days of your life;—and the next, slight, reproach, revile and attempt to confute an important article of it *? (2.) Have you suffered as much for a zealous maintenance of the intrinsic power of the church, and of Christ's sole headship over her as his spiritual kingdom, as the compilers and cordial adherers to that Confession have done? If not, modesty, as well as equity, might have restrained your revilings. (3) Suppose that, contrary to my judgment, I should allow, that magistrates *as such* have not that power relative to religious matters mentioned in our Confessions, and solemnly avowed in our Covenants, yet, being Christians, they are bound *as such* to execute their civil offices in that manner which most effectually promotes the honour and kingdom of Christ,—even as parents or masters, who are Christians, are bound to exercise their power in their families, as may best maintain and propagate the knowledge, faith, and obedience of the gospel. Every other character or office, which a Christian hath, must be subordinated to his character as a Christian.

* See the wickedness of such conduct excellently exposed in Walker's Vindication of the Discipline and Constitutions of the Church of Scotland.

1 Pet. iv. 11. Col. iii. 17. Eph. v. 21,—33. vi. 1,—9. Col. iii. 18,—25. iv. 1. 1 Tim. ii. 1, 2, 3. Tit. ii. 1,—10. iii. 2. 1 Pet. ii. 11,—20. & iii. 1,—7. Rom. xiii. (4.) If to prevent confounding of the kingdom of Christ with the kingdoms of this world, magistrates who are heads of large political families, must be excluded from all that care about religion, which is allotted them in our Confession of Faith, Heads of families, must, for the same reason, be excluded from establishing the gospel-worship of God in their houses, and from instructing their children or servants in the truths of divine revelation, at least from requiring them to attend such instructions and worship. You pretend, there is a difference; But, Sir, I insist on your stating it precisely, and proving from scripture and reason, that headship over families is a more spiritual relation than headship over multitudes of families; or, that magistrates cannot without sin, do what is similar to every thing which parents and masters, as such, are commanded to do. (5.) If, to prevent confounding of the church with the state, magistrates must exercise no care about religion,—must punish no publicly obstinate heretic, blasphemer, idolater, profaner of the Sabbath, or reviler of the oracles and ordinances of Christ, *as a criminal against the welfare of the state*,—Church-courts must censure, *as scandals against the welfare of the church*, no theft, murder, robbery, treason, unlawful war, perversion of civil judgment, or the like: as these pertain to the kingdoms of this world. (6) Though the powers of civil and ecclesiastical government be COORDINATE, each standing on its proper basis, and the right exercise of church power contributing mightily to the welfare of the state,—and of civil power to the advancement of the church,—yet they are not COLLATERAL, inseparable from, or dependent upon each other, but are altogether distinct from, and different, in many respects *.

* See this point excellently handled in the Hundred and Eleven Propositions of the Assembly, 1645. republished by Allstun, Edinburgh.

1. Civil

1. Civil and ecclesiastical power differ in their FOUNDATION. Magistracy is founded on God's universal dominion over all nations; and hence the law of nature is the *immediate supreme rule* of its administrations, and the scriptures become the rule of them only as introduced by the law of nature, requiring magistrates as well as others to believe and obey whatever revelation, duly attested, God is pleased to grant them. —or, by magistrates subjecting their consciences, as followers of Christ, to the scriptures as their only rule to direct them how to glorify God and enjoy him for ever. But ecclesiastical power is founded in the œconomical or mediatorial headship of Jesus Christ over his church, as his spiritual kingdom; and hence the immediate standard for regulating the exercise of it, is that Revelation, which God hath given to, and by him, in his word;—and the laws of nature have a regulating force in the church by virtue of the general precepts of scripture, as 1 Cor. xiv. 26, 40. vi 12. xvi. 14 Phil. iv. 8. Mat. vii. 12.

2. Civil and ecclesiastical power differ in their IMMEDIATE OBJECT. Magistratical power immediately relates only to *things external*, pertaining to the outward man. Even, when exercised about sacred things, it hath that which is *external* for its *immediate object*. It removes external hindrances of spiritual exercises, and provides external opportunities and accommodations for the performance of them. If magistrates call a Synod, they do not properly call it as *a court of Christ*, or as *ministers of Christ*, but as a meeting of subjects, whose joint deliberations are calculated to promote the honour of God the King of nations, and the happiness of their country, by the right government of the church. If a magistrate command persons to compear before a church-court to be judged, or to bear witness, he commands them not as spiritual members of Christ's mystical body, but as his own and Jehovah's subjects, to take their trial or attest the truth before proper arbitrators of their cause, that God may be honoured, and through keeping of order in the church, the welfare of the city or nation may be advanced and confirmed. If he punish insolent contemners of the authority and censures of the church,

church, he punisheth them not as *scandalous persons*, but as *criminals*, insulters of that true religion which the civil law hath established, and contemners of those judicatories which it hath authorized, and to which themselves have solemnly engaged all due subjection, —and thus, as treacherous disturbers of the good order and peace of his kingdom, and tramplers on the laws of the Most High Sovereign of the nation.—— But church-power hath that which is *spiritual* for its only proper object. It properly deals with mens *consciences and heart*, and with their outward man, only in order to affect those, in the way of conviction, reformation, comfort, *&c.* It considers the persons with whom it deals, not as *mere men*, or as *members of a civil* society, but as members of the *spiritual and mystical body of Christ*, in the visible form of it.

3. Civil and ecclesiastical power differ in their FORM. Though magistrates be the *ministers of God* for good to men, their power over their subjects is of a LORDLY nature. They are *lordly* fathers, who, by making and enforcing civil laws, can *compel* the disobedient.——In this view, if they establish any thing pertaining to the church, they establish it as a mean of honouring God their Superior, in the advancement of the welfare of the commonwealth. If they punish faults, they consider them as *crimes*, injurious to the happiness of the state, dishonouring God its supreme Governor, and provoking his wrath against it, and they punish those crimes only on the outward man, by fining, imprisonment, death, *&c.*—— But church-power is altogether MINISTERIAL, distributing to men, reproofs, admonitions, and other ordinances, according to the inspired prescriptions of Christ, Mat. xvi. 19. & xviii. 18. 1 Cor. iv. 1, 2. Christ being her alone Lord, Church-rulers have no power to make any *laws properly so called*, Isa. xxxiii. 22 James iv. 12. In dealing with offenders, they consider faults, even oppression, tyranny, sinful wars and leagues, perversion of judgment, bribery or the like in magistrates, who are members, not *as crimes*, but merely *as scandals*, defiling and ruining mens souls, plaguing the church, and dishonouring and provoking Christ and his Father in him,

him, against it. They have no *compulsory power*,—can punish no man either in his person or his external property,—can use no weapons but such as are *spiritual*, mighty through God; administring church censures, not as punishments, but as spiritual privileges, and divinely instituted means of bringing offenders to a thorough repentance of their sins, to the eternal salvation of their souls.—And this whole power must be used, only in the name of Jesus Christ, as Head of his church, 2 Cor. i. 24. x. 4, 5, 8. xiii. 8, 10. ii. 6,—10. 1 Cor, v. 4.

4. Civil and ecclesiastical power differ in their PROPER END. The *formal end of magistratical power* is to advance the glory of God, the King of nations, in promoting the welfare of the commonwealth;—and the establishment of the true religion, and care to promote the prosperity and propagation of the church, are used as eminent means of gaining that end. Or, the good of the church may also be considered as an *accessory end* of civil administration, as the better civil justice be executed, open out breakings restrained, and virtue encouraged by the magistrate, the fewer will probably be the scandals, and the greater the purity and prosperity of the church. Nay, though the advancement of the church's welfare be not the formal end of magistracy, yet as Christ is made Head over all things to his church, every magistrate, who professeth the Christian religion, ought to pursue the formal end of his office, as subordinated to his *Christian end* of promoting the glory of God in the welfare of the church and eternal salvation of men.—But the formal *end* of all church power is the glorifying of God in Christ, by promoting the spiritual conviction, conversion and edification of mens souls; and the welfare of nations is but an *accessory* or *subordinate* end, at which church-rulers, as subjects in the state, ought always to aim;—as the better they prosecute and obtain the end of their office, the fewer will be the crimes, the better both subjects and magistrates, and the more numerous and valuable the blessings of God on the nation.

5. Civil and ecclesiastical power differ in their PROPER EFFECTS. The *proper effects* of magistratical

power, rightly exercised, is the good of the commonwealth, in their commodious enjoyment of civil privileges, in a manner mightily calculated to promote the honour of God, as the Most High over all the earth;—and the purity, peace and prosperity of the church, arising from the right administration of justice, discouragement of evil doers, and praise of them that do well, is but an *accessory effect*. But the *proper effect* of church power rightly exercised, is the conversion of men to Jesus Christ, fellowship with him, and growth in grace and good works, to the praise of his glory; and the advantage accruing to cities or nations, by the virtuous laws and fervent prayers of church-members, is but an *accessory effect* of it.

6. Civil and ecclesiastical power differ in their SUBJECTS of residence. No ecclesiastical power can reside in a heathen, a woman, or a child; and no power of jurisdiction in a single person;—as civil power often may, or doth. Nor can one ecclesiastic officer delegate his power to another.

7. They differ in their FORMAL CONSIDERATION OF THE PERSONS UPON WHOM THEY ARE EXERCISED. A magistrate's power extends over all persons resident in his territory, be their moral character what it will, Jews, Heathens, &c. Rom xiii 1. But church-power extends only to the professed members of Christ's mystical body, the Church, 1 Corinth. v. 12, 13.

8. Civil and ecclesiastical power differ in respect of their DIVIDED EXERCISE. The one may, and ought to be exercised, whether the other be so or not.——The *end of church-censure* being to gain sinners to repentance and salvation, scandalous persons appearing penitent, ought to be seasonably absolved from it, and restored to communion with the church in sealing ordinances. But the *end of civil punishment* being the satisfaction of the law, and the deterring of others from the like faults, criminals, however penitent and fully restored to church-fellowship, may, as the nature of their crime demands, be punished, even unto death. And suppose a church-member should have satisfied the demands of the civil law for a crime, he ought to be prosecuted and censured for it as a scandal,

dal, by the ecclesiastical courts, till he appear duly penitent. Not only ought church-rulers to censure scandalous persons, when magistrates take no notice of their faults, but even to censure magistrates, who are church-members, for what wickedness they commit under colour of countenance from the civil law. And where magistrates punish, and church-rulers censure the same persons for the same faults, the processes ought to be kept entirely distinct from, and independent of each other;—though, to prevent unnecessary swearing, the proof taken in one court may sometimes be produced and judged of, also in the other.

OBJECT. XXII. " Magistrates not being proper judges of the doctrines of Revelation, cannot be capable to judge concerning religious matters, and particularly to determine who are heretics, blasphemers, or idolaters." ANSW. (1.) That they have a right to judge in these matters hath been already established. (2) God, who knows all things, admits private Christians to be capable of judging what is heresy, blasphemy and idolatry, and who are heretics, blasphemers and idolaters, and hence commands them to keep themselves from these sins, and to avoid such seducers, and debar them from their houses, Rom. xvi. 17. 2 Tim. iii 5. 1 Cor. v. 11. 1 John iv. 1,—3. & v. 21. 2 John 9,——11. Now what hinders Christian magistrates to have as much good sense and as much capacity of judging in these matters, as common Christians (2.) The gross errors, blasphemies and idolatries which magistrates ought to restrain, and *suitably* and *seasonably* punish, are so plainly condemned by the word of God, which magistrates ought carefully to search, under the direction of the Holy Spirit, that any unbiassed person of common capacity may easily discern them (3.) The advice of faithful ministers, and the common consent of Christian churches, may assist magistrates in discerning from the word of God, what is gross or damnable heresy, blasphemy, idolatry.

OBJECT. XXIII. " If magistrates, as such, have a power of judging in religious matters, then Heathen magistrates must also be allowed to make laws concerning religion and the church, while in the mean time they cannot be censured by the church, if they do amiss." Answ. (1.) What could you gain, if I should plead, that it is magistrates Christianity requiring them to execute their office in subordination to it, that is the immediate origin of their power about the matters of religion, even as it is parents Christianity that warrants them to receive baptism for their infants? But (2.) Heathen magistrates, with God's direction and approbation, have made laws respecting religion, Ezra vii. 13,—28. vi. 1,—14. i. 1,—3. Dan. iii. 29. vi. 26. Jonah iii. Dare you condemn the Almighty? (3.) Heathen magistrates have the same power as Christian magistrates, but are less capable to use it aright; even as heathen parents and masters have the same power over their children and servants as Christians, but are less qualified to discern and perform their duty. (4.) Neither heathen nor Christian magistrates have any power at all against the truth, but for the truth,—any power for the destruction of the church, but for her edification, 2 Cor. xiii. 8, 10. (5.) Heathen magistrates therefore, ought carefully to improve what assistance they have by the light of nature and works of creation and providence, or by any Revelation from God, to which they have access, —always taking heed to make no laws, but such as they certainly know to be agreeable to the law of God. —It is not to be expected, that civil laws can forbid every fault and require every thing good in externals; but they ought never to encourage sin, or discourage duty.

Object. XXIV. "To allow magistrates a power of judging about the matters of religion will make them church-rulers." Answ. (1) No more than it made Nebuchadnezzar, Darius, Cyrus, Darius, and Artaxerxes, and the king of Nineveh church-rulers. (2.) No more than church-rulers taking cognizance of murder, adultery, incest, theft, robbery, or even of the conduct of Christian magistrates relative to administration of justice, wars, alliances, &c. will make them magistrates. (3.) How often must you be told, that church-rulers judge, how such profession or practice ought to stand connected with ecclesiastical encouragements

couragements, discouragements or censure; but magistrates judge, how such profession or practice ought to be connected with civil encouragements or discouragements. Church-rulers warn against, and censure mens public faults, *only as scandals*, disgraceful and hurtful to the church. Magistrates judge of, and punish them *only as crimes*, hurtful to the prosperity of the State. In church courts, matters are considered as the *matters of the Lord.* In civil courts, they are considered as the *matters of the king,* 2 Chron. xix. 8,—11. Ministers as the deputies of Christ, require magistrates to execute their office for the honour of Christ, and welfare of his church, and censure them, if church-members, if they do not. Magistrates as vicegerents of God, the King of nations, require ministers faithfully to execute their office, particularly as stated by the laws of the land, in order to promote virtue and happiness among the subjects, and draw the blessing of God upon them; and they punish them *as undutiful subjects,* if they notoriously transgress, 1 Kings ii. 26. Magistrates have NO ECCLESIASTICAL POWER at all. They have no power to restrain or hinder the free and full exercise of church power. But, by giving full opportunity, encouragement and excitement to church-officers, they have power to provide that church power be freely and faithfully exercised in their dominions. They have no power to transact any thing ecclesiastical, as in admission of members into the church, or to the seals of God's covenant;—no power to choose or ordain church officers;—no power to preach the gospel, dispense the sacrament, inflict censures, or absolve from them.—— They have no power to prescribe or enact any ecclesiastical laws; but they have power to adopt such lawful and expedient constitutions, as have been made by the church-courts, into their civil code, by a legal ratification,—and power to enact such *political laws* as are necessary for the more advantageous execution of these ecclesiastical constitutions. They have no power to frame a religion for their subjects, or ratify a false religion already received or framed, or to establish any thing in religion, which is not founded in the word of God; but they have a power to adopt the law of
God

God, and the religion prescribed by it, as a part of their civil law, in order to promote the glory of God in the welfare of the nation.——The more public church courts be, and the more extensive his influence upon his subjects, and the welfare of the nation,—the more right hath the civil magistrate to exercise his *political power* about them. The church having an intrinsic right and power from Christ to call Synods for government, whenever her circumstances require it, the magistrate hath no power to deprive her of this right. But while the church calls them as courts of Christ, constituted of church rulers appointed by him to act in his name, the magistrate may call them as courts established by the civil law, and necessary to to promote the peace, order and piety, and so the prosperity of his subjects,—as courts, which consist of his principal subjects, and to which place and protection must be given in his dominions. The magistrate hath no power of deputing to Synods such members as he pleaseth, Acts xv. 2 Chron. viii. 18. or, to hinder or recal those whom the church hath deputed, unless the safety of the state plainly require it. But he may compel members, and parties who have causes before the court, to attend, if the case of the church require it, as a mean of repressing a malicious and turbulent faction, who have, or may hurt the State. It is not necessary, that either the magistrate, or his Commissioner, attend ecclesiastical Synods;—though to secure their protection, curb unruly troublers of the court, and to witness the propriety of their procedure, he may attend.——If he attend, He hath a power to judge for himself, how matters are ecclesiastically transacted,---a power *politically* to provide, That the members meddle with no political affairs, which do not belong to them as a court of Christ;---and to take care, that members, and others present, observe that due decency, in reasoning, voting, submitting, or hearing, which the nature of the court requires. If any cause be partly civil and partly ecclesiastical, he is to judge the civil part himself, and leave the ecclesiastical to the church court.——Even in ecclesiastical causes, he may give his advice, nay, he may propose and require Synods to examine and decide concerning

points

points of doctrine or practice, if necessary for the satisfaction of his own conscience, or the instruction and edification of his subjects, in order to promote the welfare of the state, in subordination to the glory of God. But he hath no power to hinder others to propose their difficulties or grievances before the Synod for satisfaction or redress, unless the cause be partly of a political nature, a Synodical decision of which, at that time, endangers the state.—He hath no power to preside in the Synod, or give his decisive vote in any of their transactions. But, as a man and Christian, he hath right to a *judgment of discretion*, Whether their decisions be according to the law of God or not, — and as a magistrate, he hath a power of *political judgment*, by which he doth not properly judge, Whether these decisions be true or false, good or bad in themselves, but Whether, and How far, they ought to be ratified, and as it were adopted into the laws of the State, and connected with civil rewards, forbearance, or punishments. Thus, the power of the magistrate, *in nothing* interferes with the power of the Synod. Nothing is done by the one, as a magistrate, that the other can do, as a court of Christ. And as the decisions of Synods are *supreme in the ecclesiastic order*, from which there is no appeal but to Jesus Christ;—By remonstrating as a church-member, and commanding them as their King, the magistrate may cause the Synod re-consider its own deeds, but he cannot reverse them himself;—so the magistrate's deed concerning the civil ratification of church-deeds is *supreme in its kind*, from which there is no appeal but to God himself. The Synod may require him as a Church-member; and, as subjects, they may remonstrate, and supplicate his re-consideration of his own deed, but they cannot reverse it themselves.

OBJECT. XXV. " To allow magistrates to judge in matters of religion for others, and to restrain and punish corruptions in it, is to render them Lords of mens faith and conscience,—a power which even the inspired apostles disclaimed. For if magistrates impose any religion at all upon their subjects, it must be what their own conscience dictates; and then what shall become of the private rights of conscience, among their subjects?" Answ. (1.) Did then God, who of old commanded magistrates to judge about matters of religion, and to restrain and punish blasphemers, idolaters, seducers, profaners of the Sabbath, Deut. xiii. 9, 10. & xvii. 5,---7. Lev. xxiv. 11,---14. Song ii. 15. Num. xv. 32,---36. command them to lord it over mens conscience? If it was not so then, it cannot be so now, as conscience, tyranny and murder, are the same in every age. (2.) The objection strikes with equal force, against all ecclesiastical establishment of the true religion, and against all creeds and Confessions of Faith, and against all ecclesiastical judging and censuring of men for heresy, blasphemy, or idolatry, contrary to Rev. ii. 20. Titus iii. 10. Gal. v. 10, 11. as against magistrates judging about establishing religion or punishing the public insulters of it. (3.) Magistrates act in this matter as *his ministers* and vicegerents, by virtue of his commandment, who is the alone Lord of conscience, and restrain or punish nothing, but what men, under any proper influence of faith and conscience, would abstain from, as forbidden by the Lord of conscience, who is to be their future judge, and hath appointed magistrates, as his substitutes to avenge the open injuries done to him in this world, Rom. xiii. 4. And, if men persist in sins plainly forbidden in his law, he holds them as sinners against, and condemned by their conscience, Tit. iii. 10, 11. (4.) The absurdity of mens consciences being sustained as a standard, as well as the proper method of magistrates making laws relative to religion, have been already manifested. Magistrates consciences have no more just claim to God head than those of their meanest subjects. Not, therefore, magistrates pretences to conscience, but plain and evident marks of the authority of God manifested in, and from the scriptures, must determine their subjects to receive a religion in obedience to their authority, as subordinated to the authority of God, the Most High, superior of both.

Object. XXVI. "In Rom. xiii. where the power of magistrates is more fully described than any where else in the New Testament, only the commands of the second

second table of the moral law are subjoined, to mark that it only extends to the concerns of men one with another." ANSW. (1.) Who authorized the objector to put asunder the two Testaments and the two tables which God hath joined? Or, to separate the first part of that chapter from the last, which certainly relates to religion, any more than from verse 9th. (2.) The magistrate's character, *minister of God for good, terror to, and revenger of evil doers*, and his duty to love his neighbours as himself there hinted, cannot admit of his having no care about religion and the first table of the moral law. (3.) To oblige men carefully to search the whole scriptures, God hath seldom, if ever, manifested his whole will, relative to any thing, in one passage.

OBJECT. XXVII. "If we allow magistrates any power at all about religious matters, we must plunge ourselves into inextricable difficulties, as the precise limits of civil and ecclesiastical power can never be fixed,—and every small mistake in religious opinions, or neglect of religious duties, must bring men to the gibbet, as theft draws down the wrath of God on nations, as well as blasphemy and idolatry do." ANSW. There is no more difficulty in limiting the power of magistrates about either religion or virtue, than in fixing precise limits to the power of church-rulers relative to those matters. Do you fix precise limits to church-power according to the word of God, and I shall next moment fix as precise limits for the power of the magistrate. If you limit the exercise of church power to duties required, and sins forbidden in the first table of the moral law,—you naturally leave the care of the duties required in the second table to the magistrate. But then, whether a church of Christ, having no care or power about morality toward men, —or a deputed kingdom of God without any care or power about any thing relating to the honour of God, be most absurd and devilish, I know not. If you aver, That the power of church-rulers extends to the external obedience or disobedience of church-members to both tables of God's law, not as *civil*, but as *spiritual* conduct, tending to the spiritual advantage or hurt of the church, and therefore connected with the spiritual encouragements or frowns of Christ's visible church; and that they meddle not with sins against the second table *as crimes* against mens person or property, but *as scandals* against the spiritual edification of the church, and the glory of Jesus Christ therein concerned;—I immediately reply, That precisely, in like manner, the power of magistrates extends to the external obedience or disobedience of *civil subjects as such*, to both tables of God's law, *not as it is of a spiritual nature*, but *as it affects the civil welfare or hurt of the nation*, or honour of God as the King of it, and so ought to stand connected with civil encouragements or discouragements. If you pretend, that it will be still hard to shew, how far magistrates may, in that view, proceed in matters of the first table, particularly with respect to offending clergymen. I answer, that it is not one whit harder, than to shew how far church courts may proceed in matters of the second table, particularly with respect to offensive magistratical administrations. (2.) Your pretence, that if magistrates punish any faults in religion, they must punish all known faults in the same form and degree, is but a deceitful insult on the Most High, who, in his word, appointed the capital punishment of idolaters and blasphemers, and yet never warranted the punishment of many faults relative to religion, in like manner; nay, for ought I see, hath not required magistrates at all to punish any thing but the most atrocious faults in it. If you insult Christ, who hath not commanded any faults, but atrocious ones obstinately continued in, to be censured with excommunication, and hath never commanded many lesser neglects and infirmities of church-members to be censured at all,—It is an insult on common sense. Would you, or any man in his wits, either censure or punish men *as severely* for a simple neglect of a religious duty, as for an open and blasphemous insulting of religion? Would you censure or punish the stealing of a single straw as severely as the stealing of a man or woman? Would you censure or punish a prick with a pin, as severely as the cutting of a man's throat, or the ripping up of a woman with child.

OBJECT.

OBJECT. XXVIII. " Either every error in doctrine, and mistake in worship must be punished by the magistrate, or only that which is more glaring and notorious. If it is only the latter, How are the limits of what is punishable, and what is not, and the degree of punishment proper for each, to be precisely fixed."
ANSW. If every species of duty must be neglected, and the contrary sin allowed, where it is difficult to fix the precise boundaries of sin or duty,—or where it is difficult to fix the precise degrees of encouragement to be given to such obedience, or of censure or punishment due to such sin, men must be left to live like absolute atheists, in both church and state, every man doing that which is right in his own eyes. (2) Unless you prove that every insult of, and outrage against God and his religion ought to pass unpunished, and even be licensed and authorized, yourself must be equally embarrassed in fixing what is punishable and what is not, and what must be the form and degree of punishment annexed to each punishable fault. (3.) Nay, unless you prove, that all deeds, however horrid, ought to be tolerated in both church and state, How are you to fix precisely, what deeds are censurable or punishable, and what not ;—and what form and degree of censure or punishment is proper for each, in every particular form and circumstance. A man may as really, and for ought men can prove against him, as justly pretend conscience for his wicked deeds of treason, murder, robbery, &c. as for his damnable heresies, blasphemies, and idolatrous worship. Wicked deeds, if God be true, are the native fruits of gross errors and idolatrous worship. A conscience, which under the clear light of scripture revelation, approves the whole system of Popery or Socinianism, may as reasonably dictate the murder of saints, dethronement of lawful Sovereigns, community of women and goods, &c. Let once the plea of conscience be admitted in the case of treason, theft, robbery, murder, and the like, and I will undertake, it shall be as commonly pled, as in the case of gross heresy, blasphemy and idolatry ; and it will be as impossible for judges to disprove it in the one case, as in the other. Nothing therefore, will truly answer your tole-

rant scheme, but that every man be allowed to profess, worship, and act as he pleaseth. (4) Let therefore magistrates, as well as church-rulers, in their punishing and censuring work, make God's word their rule; and if they do not perceive from it clearly the proper degrees of punishment and censure, let them rather err on the charitable side, than in approaches to severity.

OBJECT. XXIX. "But, how are heretics, blasphemers, and idolaters to be got judged in order to punishment? They must be judged only by their Peers, by persons of the same station as themselves, quite impartial, and no wise attached to the contrary sentiments or practices." ANSW. (1) But, how can you prove from scripture or reason, that such criminals must be judged only by their Peers;—or that there is a nation under heaven, in which criminals are judged by such Peers, as you mention? (2) Allowing that our juries consist of the proper Peers of the criminals, yet they judge not concerning the relevancy of the crime, or the form or degree of punishments, but of the proof of the fact,—which, in the case of heresy, blasphemy, or idolatry, is ordinarily no more difficult, than in the case of adultery, incest, theft, murder, &c. (3) Nothing can be more absurd, than to pretend, that mens detestation of heresy, blasphemy, and idolatry, disqualifies them from judging heretics, blasphemers, and idolaters. What! Doth mens abhorrence of theft, murder, adultery, disqualify them to judge of, and punish those crimes? Do God's infinite holiness and equity, disqualify him from judging of sinners?

OBJECT. XXX. "If heretics, blasphemers and idolaters be punishable, orthodox magistrates, who happen to become governors of heretical, blasphemous and idolatrous nations, must kill the most of their subjects." ANSW. We hold none punishable, especially in any severe manner, till they appear openly obstinate in it, notwithstanding sufficient means of conviction, which these subjects are not supposed to have had; and so are not punishable at all by magistrates. (2.) Nothing, and particularly the infliction of punishment, ought to be done, merely because it

is

is lawful, till it also become expedient, 1 Cor. vi. 12 &
x. 23. Eccl. iii. 1, 11. Now it would be highly inexpedient to proceed to extremities against the greater part of a society. Nay, in the case supposed, they would prove a barbarously sinful mean of prejudicing men against the gospel of Christ. (3.) Great difference ought to be made between such as were never reformed from a false religion, and those who obstinately apostatize from the true religion to a false one; —between such as live in a nation generally corrupted with a false religion, and those who live in a nation generally enlightened and reformed by the gospel of Christ;—and between such as are only seduced, and those who exert themselves to seduce others. Much more forbearance is due to the former than to the latter; for (4.) However peremptorily the Jews were commanded by God to punish even unto death, the obstinate false prophets, idolaters and blasphemers of their own church or nation, they were never required to punish their idolatrous tributaries in their conquered countries of Syria, Philistia, Edom, Ammon, or Moab. And meanwhile, were never allowed, and never did grant them any *legal establishment or authoritative toleration* of their idolatry. (5.) Even God himself, for the ends of his glory, exerciseth much forbearance towards heretics, blasphemers and idolaters, but never grants them any *legal establishment or authoritative toleration*, securing them of protection in their wickedness. Let magistrates, who are *his ministers for good* to men, go and do so likewise.

OBJECT. XXXI. "The Christian law of doing to others that which we would have them do to us, demands, That we should allow every man to think, profess, and act in religion as he pleaseth. If we think men heretics, blasphemers or idolaters, our proper method is to manifest the utmost kindness and familiarity to them, that we may gain them to the truth. Every other method is no less dangerous than uncharitable. If orthodox Christian magistrates restrain and punish the spreading of Heathen, Mahometan, and Popish errors or worship,—Heathen, Mahometan and Popish princes will be thereby tempted to restrain and punish the spread of gospel truth in their dominions,
and

and can plead the very same right for their conduct."
Answ. (1.) Strange! Did not God know the meaning of his own law of equity and kindness between man and man, and the true method of securing or propagating his own religion, when he made or encouraged the laws against seducers, idolaters, and blasphemers above mentioned;—when he commanded his people to avoid false teachers, and not so much as to lodge them in their houses. (2.) With all your pretended benevolence, Would you familiarly lodge in your family a notorious pick pocket or an harlot, along with your own children, in order to gain them to the ways of piety and virtue? You would not. Why then, in direct contradiction to the command of God, do you plead for familiarity with robbers of God, defilers, or murderers of souls! (3) The Christian law of kindness and equity requires me to do all that for the real welfare of my neighbour, in subordination to the glory of God which I could lawfully wish him, in like circumstances, to do for me? But, must I do evil that good may come, rendering my damnation just? Must I procure my just liberty to believe and serve God according to his own appointment, by granting my neighbour an unjust, an authoritative licence to insult and blaspheme God, and worship the devil in his stead? Because I wish my neighbour to be helpful to me, in honouring God, and in labouring to render myself and others happy in time and eternity, Must I assist and encourage them in horribly dishonouring God, and destroying themselves and others. None but an atheist, who believes no real difference between moral good and evil, can pretend it. (4.) When and Where have faithful adherents to gospel-truth, got much liberty and safety by means of their friends encouraging and protecting gross heresy, blasphemy and idolatry? Since Protestants became so kind to Papists in their dominions, Have not the Popish powers, in return, cruelly murdered, banished, or oppressed their Protestant subjects, in Hungary, Poland, Germany, France, &c. till they have left few of them remaining? While Britons were lavishly expending their blood and treasure in support of the Popish house of Austria about 1709 and 1741, She

returned

returned our kindness in the most villanous destruction of about 230 Congregations of our Protestant brethren in Silesia and Hungary. (5.) Ought Elijah to have spared, nay protected and encouraged the prophets of Baal, as a mean of securing for himself the protection of Ahab and Jezebel, or, because she was disposed to avenge their death? Must thieves and robbers be benevolently used, protected and suffered to pass unpunished, for fear of provoking their associates to revenge the just severities used towards them? Let magistrates do their duty, and leave events to God. (6.) Till you honestly profess yourself an atheist, who believes no *intrinsical difference between moral good and evil*, never pretend that magistrates, who have their whole power from God, have any power against the truth, or have a right to exercise that power derived from God for the good of mankind, to his dishonour and to the hurt of mankind. Astonishing! Because a power originating from God may be rightfully exercised in promoting his declarative glory, the spread or protection of his gospel, and the happiness of mankind,—May it, must it, therefore, in the hand of other magistrates, be rightfully exercised in promoting blasphemy and robbery of God, and worshipping of devils?—Because it may be rightfully exercised in punishing obstinate and notorious heretics, blasphemers and idolaters,—May it, must it, therefore be rightfully exercised in persecuting and murdering the faithful preachers and professors of Gospel-truths, and worshippers of the true God?——Because magistrates in Britain have a right to punish thieves and murderers, must these in France have as good a right to use Alms-givers and skilful and diligent Physicians in the same manner?——Because that which tends to the highest honour of God, and temporal and eternal happiness of mankind ought to be authoritatively tolerated, nay established, every where,—may,—must, that which tends to his highest dishonour, and the most dreadful temporal and eternal ruin of mankind, be every where, in like manner, tolerated or established?——Because in a dearth, benevolent persons may be tolerated, nay highly encouraged in freely distributing wholsome provisions to the poor and needy, may,

or

or must, malicious murderers be therefore tolerated and encouraged in distributing their poisoned morsels, especially if abundantly sweetened among the unwary infants or others? (7.) The restraint or *suitable* and *seasonable* punishment of that which is contrary to God's law, being commanded by himself, can never have any tendency to introduce corruptions in religion, or persecution for an adherence to gospel-truth. And if some will abuse their power, that must not hinder others, either in church or state, to use theirs aright.

OBJECT. XXXII. "If infidelity and difference in religion do not make void magistrates right to govern nations, much less can heresy, idolatry, or blasphemy, invalidate subjects right to protection, or of admission to all the privileges of other subjects." ANSW. (1.) In almost every case, the restraint or punishment of superiors is more difficult than that of inferiors. (2.) If the professors of the true religion be the minority in number and power, both scripture and reason demand their subjection to their common rulers, in all their lawful commands, till they become manifest tyrants, and Providence afford a proper opportunity of shaking off their yoke. But, if the professors of the true religion be the majority in a nation or society, both scripture and reason forbid their setting up a magistrate of a false religion, or a wicked practice,—and allow that, if after his advancement, he apostatize, and obstinately attempt to promote a false religion, or notoriously wicked practice, he may be deposed and even punished, as far as the general welfare of the society, in subordination to the glory of God, can admit, Psal. xv. 4. (3.) Do you pretend to be wiser than God himself? Without any apprehended inconsistency, he commanded the Jews, not *authoritatively to tolerate*, protect, and encourage, but to punish blasphemers, profaners of the Sabbath, idolaters, and false prophets, Lev. xxiv. 15, 16 Num. xv. 35, 36. Deut. xiv, xvii. Zech. xiii. 2,—6. and yet commanded them when they were the small minority in the Chaldean empire, to serve the Heathen king of Babylon, Jer. xxvii. 17. & xxix. 7.

OBJECT.

OBJECT. XXXIII. "Unlimited tolerations in the state ought not to be granted. In Protestant countries, Papists ought not to be tolerated, as they are subject to the foreign power of the Pope, as their Head, and cannot be supposed faithful subjects to, or to keep faith with such as they pretend to be heretics. Atheists ought not to be tolerated, as they cannot be bound by any oath. Such as are against tolerating others ought not to be tolerated, as they will kindle strife. And in churches, there ought to be no toleration at at all." ANSW. (1.) Then it seems, Christ and his Father must be excluded from all share in the toleration you plead for, on account of their intolerant disposition, unless they be infinitely altered from what they were in antient times (2.) You have already given up all your care for procuring the favour of the Popish powers to your Protestant brethren abroad, by means of tolerating Papists. (3.) Never pretend zeal against atheism, till you be able to maintain your *tolerant* scheme, upon other than the atheistical principles mentioned near the beginning of this missive; and to which you have had repeated recourse in your objections,—and till you allow mens rights or pretences of conscience to warrant them to defame, abuse, rob, and murder yourself, as you allow with respect to God. (4.) Your present objection is partly founded in atheism. Papists are excluded from toleration, not at all as notorious blasphemers and idolaters, but merely as not very like to prove faithful subjects to Protestant magistrates: Atheists are excluded, not as daring blasphemers or intentionally malicious murderers of Jehovah, but merely because they cannot give proper security for their good behaviour to magistrates and fellow subjects. Thus no more regard is shewed to God the *King of nations*, than might be expected among a nation of Atheists, and the interests of men are altogether, I might say, infinitely, preferred to his. (5.) How are you to fix the *precise limits*, Who are to be accounted under foreign heads;—who are to be accounted Papists and Atheists;—or who are to be held to give sufficient security by oath,—Whether profane swearers, Quakers, Socinians, notorious violaters of baptismal engagements, solemn subscribers of, and engagers to Creeds and Confessions of Faith which they believe not, &c.—If, contrary to the light of nature and revelation, men zealously propagate the doctrines of devils and do worship them in idols, and follow the pernicious practices above-mentioned, as the native consequences of error and idolatry, Are not they plainly subject to another Head, even the God of this world, who is not much more friendly to magistrates and nations, than the Romish Pope? If men have conscience, villainously to wrest the scripture to prove that Christ was originally a *mere man*, a *mere creature*, and is now a *made God*, What more security can we have by their oath, than if they were professed Atheists? (6.) None who plead for the *authoritative toleration* of heretics, blasphemers and idolaters by the State, can with any self-consistent candor, disallow of all toleration in the church.——God the King of nations, hates these abominations as much as Christ, the Head of the church. Church-rulers have no other infallible rule to direct them in their decisions, than magistrates have. They are as unfit to judge of more refined errors, as magistrates are to judge of gross errors, blasphemies, idolatries. They have as little allowance from Christ to lord over mens consciences, or to impose their own opinions for articles of faith or rules of duty, as magistrates have from God. It is as difficult to fix precisely, What is *censurable*, and what not, and the *proper degree of censure* answerable to every scandal, in every circumstance, as to fix precisely, what and how crimes ought to be punished by the magistrate. Unrighteous censures for an adherence to truth and duty, are as *real* and *more severe persecution* than unrighteous punishments. Articles and Confessions of Faith imposed by ecclesiastical authority, as much cramp Christian liberty, as if they were established by the state. Clergymen have as often abused their power about religion, as ever Statesmen did. Their constitutions and councils have done as much hurt to it, as those of magistrates ever did: If it be difficult to get gross heretics, blasphemers and idolaters judged, restrained or punished by the State, it will be found as hard to get ALL errors and ALL practical mistakes censured by the church. Nay, for once

once that magistrates have erred in punishing heretics, blasphemers and idolaters, I believe clergymen have erred ten, if not an hundred times, in their censures. And, seldom have ever magistrates persecuted men for righteousness sake, but when they were instigated to it by some clergymen.

OBJECT. XXXIV. "No carnal influence of magistrates relative to religion is consistent with the spiritual nature of the kingdom of Christ, which is not of this world, John xviii. 36. The apostles used no carnal weapons of warfare in promoting it, 2 Cor. x. 4, 5." ANSW. Why do not you state precisely, what you mean by the *spiritual nature* of Christ's kingdom, and its not being *of this world?* Is it *so spiritual*, that the members and subordinate rulers in it, are not at the same time members in a civil state, and interested in the welfare or hurt of it? Is it *so spiritual*, that it hath no manner of connexion or fellowship with the kingdom of God over the nation, in which it resides, and neither gives nor receives from it, any more helpfulness, than from the kingdom of Belial? Is it *so spiritual*, that the power of it cannot touch any part of mens conduct toward one another, or even the magistratical administrations of its members? Is it *so spiritual*, as to exclude the Most High, King of nations, and his deputed vicegerents, from all regard to the honour of God and his religion, and the welfare of the State as connected therewith, leaving them no more concern therewith, than if nations were herds of swine? The question under consideration is not concerning the nature of Christ's kingdom, of which the civil magistrate is not a ruler of any kind, as hath been already manifested, but, Whether all care about the church and her religion, as tending to promote the welfare of nations ought to be excluded from *God's kingdom*, as the *Sovereign of nations*, and he and his vicegerents obliged to manage that department, as if there were no God in the earth? (2.) Had Christ no *spiritual kingdom* in the days of Moses, and the prophets, when God required magistrates to take care about religion, and to restrain and punish the public atrocious insulters of it? Had he *no spiritual kingdom*, not of this world, when he repeatedly drove the buyers and sellers out of the temple? (3.) That the spiritual nature of Christ's kingdom rendered it perfectly consistent with the full exercise of the magistratical power in the Roman empire, or any other state, which is what he meant in his answer to Pilate, we readily grant; but the inspired promises, which have been repeatedly quoted, Isa. xlix. 23. & lx. 3, 10. 16 Psal. ii. 8, 10, 11, 12. & lxxii. 10, 11. Rev. xi. 15. & xvii 16. & xxi. 24. sufficiently prove, that the spiritual nature of Christ's kingdom doth not exclude magistrates helpfulness to the truth, in authorizing the profession and practice of it by their civ'l laws, and in restraining the open and insolent blasphemers of it? (4.) Though the weapons of ministers warfare, in propagating the gospel be not carnal, What is that to the case of magistrates? And as the spiritual weapons of church officers reach as much to sins against the second table of the moral law as to those against the first, they no more exclude the use of the magistrates carnal weapons against the atrocious sins against the first table, than with respect to those against the second, 2 Cor. x. 6. 1 Cor. v. 2,—5, (4.) Magistratical influence cannot set up Christ's kingdom in mens heart, or oblige mens conscience to obey his laws in an acceptable manner; but it can remove many external hindrances, and afford many external opportunities, of his own setting up, by means of his word and Spirit. It can restrain burning of Bibles or abusing and murdering of preachers and hearers of the gospel. It can spread the scriptures, and protect preachers of the truths contained in them; and by command, example, and otherwise, encourage the subjects to search the scriptures, and to hear, learn, profess, and practise the plain doctrines of the gospel. In thus endeavouring to make their subjects attend on, receive, and observe the doctrines of the gospel, all *appearance of force* should be carefully avoided, as that is apt to provoke a dislike, rather than to promote a chearful embracement of them. But force may be used to restrain, or *duly* and *seasonably* punish the insolent opposers and revilers of the true religion, which is established. And, on no account, ought such plagues of nations

nations, as well as of churches, to receive any authoritative *licence* to commit such wickedness.

OBJECT. XXXV. "The annexing of temporal encouragements to the profession and practice of the Christian religion or external discouragements to the profession or practice of such opinions and worship as are contrary to it,—tends to render men hypocrites, and their religion merely carnal, in obedience to civil authority, and influenced by mere carnal motives. It makes men trample on and *debauch* their conscience, and so *sap the foundation of all true piety* and *virtue.*"

ANSW. (1.) God, who well knows the true nature of religious worship and obedience, and highly regards the candor and purity of conscience, excited the Israelites to it, partly by external encouragements, restraints and terrors, Deut. iv.,—viii, xxvii,—xxxii, Lev. xviii,—xx, xxvi. and by each of his prophets, Isa. i.——to Mal. iv. And even under the gospel, godliness hath the *promises of this life,* as well as of that which is to come, 1 Tim iv. 8. 1 Pet. iii. 13.—— Did you mean to blaspheme his conduct as absolutely devilish? (2.) With God's approbation, David, Nehemiah and others, by familiar intimacy, and by preferring them to posts of honour, encouraged such as appeared eminent in the profession and practice of revealed religion; and they excluded such as appeared notoriously wicked, Psal. cxix. 63. & ci. 6, 7. Neh. vii 2. & xiii, 28. Nay, David before hand publicly intimated his resolution to prefer only pious and faithful men.—And why not, when such bid fairest to be eminently useful officers in the state? (3) Why may not men, even by external advantages be encouraged to an external attendance upon gospel-ordinances, which, by the blessing of God and the working of his Spirit, may issue in rendering them eminently useful subjects, and in their eternal salvation, even as children may be hired to that reading of their Bible and learning of their Catechism, which may issue in their conversion and everlasting life? (4) Regard to the command of parents, masters, magistrates, and ministers, all at once, in our religious profession and practice, is no way inconsistent with, but may be delightfully subordinated to a supreme regard to the authority

rity of God in them. (5.) Do you really think, that those, who believe neither a God, nor a heaven, nor a hell, ought under pretence of civil right, to be as readily admitted to places of power and trust, in civil governments as the most pious?—Nay, are not even a profession and practice of the Christian religion much more profitable in a nation, than open blasphemy, impiety and idolatry, which we have heard from God's own word, exceedingly corrupt mens morals, and pull down the wrath of God on the society. (6.) If such things only be restrained and punished, as are plainly contrary to the law of God, and a right conscience, and never punished, till after sufficient means of conviction have been afforded and trampled on, how can that make men dissemble with or sin against their conscience, any more than the punishment of theft, murder, incest, or the like, can do it?

OBJECT. XXXVI. "The abolishment of all civil establishments of revealed religion, would have a remarkable tendency to render men truly pious, truly sincere, in their faith, profession and worship; and to render them excellent subjects, candid, peaceable, and affectionate lovers of one another. It would effectually root out Popery and every thing similar." ANSW. (1.) Just as remarkable a tendency, as the leaving of children to themselves hath to render them truly virtuous, and a distinguished honour to their parents, Prov. xxv. 15. 1 Sam. iii. 13.—as remarkable a tendency as the abolishment of all ecclesiastical establishments of it would have to render men perfect saints. (2.) It is plain, that God, when he fixed a civil establishment of revealed religion, and when he represented, as above, heresy, blasphemy, and idolatry, as rendering men monsters of all manner of wickedness, instead of *good subjects*, neighbours, or Christians, thought otherwise. Are you wiser than He? (3.) Never, that I know of, was there a nation or numerous society on earth, in which there was less of a religious establishment, good or bad, than among the Ismaelians of Irak and Syria, and the Giagas of Africa. What were the noted virtues which flourished among them? Murders, assassinations, which cannot be read or heard, without horror. Under the protection of *of Heresy, Blasphemy, &c. answered* 89

an extensive toleration, how did England, about an hundred and thirty years ago, swarm with Sectarian errors, blasphemies, confusions ? And, what hath either the peace of the State, or the orthodoxy and holiness of our church gained by our last Scotch toleration ? Repeated attempts in 1715 and 1745, to unhinge our civil establishment and dethrone our lawful Sovereigns in favours of Popish pretenders, are the noted advantages, which have accrued to our State, and an alarming increase of infidelity, profaneness, and Popery, to our church. Instead of scarce six hundred Papists, which was once all that could be reckoned in Scotland, their number now, may amount to about thirty thousand. In about a dozen of parishes in the North, they have above twenty congregations, several of them pretty large, and a College and an Academy for training up priests. How quickly these, with the Scotch colleges abroad, may furnish converters for the whole nation, God only knows. In the parish of South Uist, there are 2300 Papists and 300 Protestants; in Barra 1250 Papists, and 50 Protestants; in Ardnamurchan 1950 Papists, and 17 Protestants; in Kirkmichael and its neighbouring parish 1520 Papists ; in Kilmanivaig 1600 ; and in Glenelg 1340.

OBJECT. XXXVII. " All civil laws establishing revealed religion must necessarily land magistrates in *persecuting* their subjects ; for, if these civil laws be contemned and violated, the breakers must be punished " ANSW. For this reason no superior, parent, master, minister, or magistrate, must make any appointment relative to religious matters, because, if it be disregarded, punishment or censure must be inflicted, and that will amount to persecution in the sense of the objection.——No duty must ever be attempted, lest some perplexing consequence should attend it. (2.) Tho' *evil doers* ordinarily reckon restraints of iniquity *persecution*, the scripture allows nothing to be *persecution* but unjust severities exercised against the profession or practice of gospel-truth,—at least against innocence or virtue Punishment of men for what is plainly contrary to the word of God is no persecution for conscience sake, but a proper correction of them for trampling on and murdering their conscience.

ence. (3.) If, by the blessing of God, parents can do much to advance religion in their families, without any furious or hurtful beating of their children,—and ministers do much to promote it in their congregations, without proceeding, perhaps once in their life, to the higher excommunication; and if both may do much to render their children and people useful members of the commonwealth, without having power to fine, imprison or kill them, why may not magistrates by their appointments, encouragements, and example, much promote the profession and practice of revealed religion, without proceeding, unless very rarely, to any disagreeable severities?——The point we attempted directly to establish is, that *magistrates ought never to grant an authoritative toleration to gross heresy, blasphemy, idolatry:* you therefore act uncandidly in perpetually haling in the affair of punishments; even capital ones, just as your tolerant friends the antient Remonstrants perpetually haled in the doctrine of reprobation, in order to render the sovereignty of God's grace odious to the people. (4) If magistrates take heed never to punish on the head of religious matters, but when the CRIME is plainly relevant and manifest, plainly contrary to the laws of God, as well as to those of the land; and that the punishment be SUITABLE and SEASONABLE, circumstantially calculated to promote the real welfare of the commonwealth, why should they be charged with persecution, for prudently supporting their most important laws, and yet held innocent, if not virtuous, in supporting their comparatively insignificant laws, relative to fishing, fowling, hunting, or the like?

OBJECT. XXXVIII. "Let things be reduced to practice. What could be done, just now, in Britain, without an *authoritative toleration* of the different parties in religion." ANSW. No difficulty of the performance of duties can be a sufficient reason for the neglect of them. No difficulty of rectifying what is in disorder, can be a proof that it is not duty to attempt it. Because I find it so hard work to keep my heart with all diligence, and often know not how to get its sinful disorders rectified, it will not follow, that to obtain inward quietness, I should, in God's name, give an authoritative toleration to my several lusts, except perhaps the grosser ones of malice, whoredom, drunkenness. (2.) The rules of rectifying what pertains to religion in Britain, is plain. Let magistrates and subjects impartially and earnestly search the oracles of God, depending on the illuminating influence of his Spirit.—Let every thing not contained in the scripture be thrown out of both civil and ecclesiastical establishments of religion, and every thing plainly appointed therein for the gospel church, be authorized. Let the whole administration of government in church and state, and subjection to it, be regulated by the law of God. -Let every prudent and winning method be taken to promote an universally chearful compliance.--If any continue to dissent, let *every degree and form of tender forbearance* be exercised towards them, which the express laws of God will permit, especially, if by a circumspect life, they manifest themselves persons of a truly tender conscience, with respect to what they apprehend.——If all will not concur in these measures, let particular persons, in their several stations, act as becometh the gospel of Christ, obeying God rather than man, and doing all that he hath commanded, without turning aside to the right-hand or to the left. And if need be, let them take up their cross, and patiently follow Christ counting nothing too dear unto them, if they may uprightly finish their course with joy.——Upon trial, it would be found as easy for magistrates to rectify the disorders in their department, relative to religion, as it would be for church-rulers in Britain, to rectify what pertains to theirs, in which, you just now pled, that there never should be any toleration at all.

OBJECT. XXXIX. "The great Dr. OWEN zealously pled for authoritative toleration, and that magistrates ought not to interfere with religious matters."

ANSW. We call no man master. One is our master even Christ. Dr. Owen's authority would be too light to balance that of many thousands of Protestant divines. But let us hear his judgment, for ought I know his FINAL JUDGMENT, in his Sermon before the English Parliament, OCTOBER 13th, 1652.——

M

"The civil powers—shall be disposed of, into an useful subserviency to the interest, power, and kingdom of Jesus Christ; hence they are said to be *his kingdoms*, Rev. xi. 15*. Judges and Rulers AS SUCH must *kiss the Son* and own his sceptre and advance his ways. Some think, if you were well settled, you ought not, *as rulers of the nations*, to put forth your power for the interest of Christ. *The good Lord keep your hearts* from that apprehension †. It is the duty of magistrates to *seek the good, peace*, and prosperity of the people committed to their charge, and to prevent and remove EVERY THING, that will bring confusion, destruction and desolation upon them, Esther x. 3. Psal. ci. Magistrates are the *ministers of God for good*—UNIVERSAL GOOD of them, to whom they are given, Rom. xiii. 4. and are to watch and apply themselves to *this very thing*, ver. 6.—It is incumbent on them to act, even as *kings and men in authority*, that we may lead a quiet and peaceable life in *all godliness* and honesty,—and all may *come to the knowledge of the truth*, 1 Tim. ii. 1,—4 ——They are to feed the people committed to their charge, with all their might, unto *universal* peace and welfare ——The things opposite to the good of any nation and people, are of two sorts ; (1.) Such as are really, directly, and immediately opposed to that state wherein they close together, and find prosperity,—seditions, tumults, disorders,—violent or fraudulent breaking in upon the privileges and enjoyments of singular persons, *without any consideration of him who ruleth all things*.—— Such evils as these, nations and rulers, *supposed to be atheists*, would, with all their strength, labour to prevent.——(2.) Such as are *morally* and *meritoriously* opposed to their good and welfare, in that they will *certainly pluck down the judgments and wrath of God* upon that nation, where they are practised and *allowed*, Rom. i. Shall he be thought a magistrate to *bear out the name, authority, and presence of God* to men, that, so he and his people have present peace like a herd of swine, cares not though such things as will certainly devour their strength, and then utterly consume them,

* Page 15. † P. 16.

do

do pass current.——Seeing they that rule over men must be just, *ruling in the fear of the Lord*, the sole reason why they sheathe the sword of justice in the bowels of thieves, murderers, adulterers, is not, *because their outward peace is actually disturbed by them*—but *principally because he*, in whose stead they stand and minister, *is provoked by such wickedness to destroy* both the one and the other. And, if there be the *same reason* concerning other things, they also call for the same procedure.——To gather up now what hath been spoken; Considering the gospel's right to be propagated with all its concernments in every nation under heaven, and the *blessings, peace, prosperity*, and *protection*, wherewith it is attended, when and where received, and the *certain destruction* which accompanies the *rejection* and *contempt* of it.—Considering the duty, that, by God's appointment is incumbent on them that rule over men, That *in the fear of the Lord* they ought to seek the good, peace, and prosperity of them that are committed to their charge, and to prevent, obviate, remove, and revenge that which tends to their hurt, perturbation, destruction, immediate from heaven, or from the hand of men ; and in their whole administration to take care, that the *worshippers of God in Christ* may lead a quiet and peaceable life *in all godliness* and honesty. Let any one, who hath the least sense of the account, which he must—make to the the great King and Judge of the world,—of the authority and power wherewith he was intrusted, determine, Whether it be not incumbent on him, by *all the protection* he can afford ; by *all the privileges* he can indulge ; by *all the support* he can grant ; by *all that encouragement* he is required or allowed to give to any person whatsoever,—to further the propagation of the gospel, which upon the matter, is the only thing of concernment, as well unto this life, as unto that which is to come.——And, if *any thing be allowed* in a nation, which, *in God's esteem*, may amount to a contempt and despising thereof, men may be taught by sad experience, what will be the issue of such ALLOWANCE* Although the institutions and examples of the Old Testament, of the duty of magistrates in the

things

* P. 49, 50.

things about the worship of God, are not, in their *whole* latitude and extent, to be drawn into rules—obligatory to all magistrates, now under—the gospel,—yet doubtless, there is something moral in these institutions.——Subduct from these administrations, what was proper to the church and nation of the Jews, and what remains upon the general account of a church and nation, must be everlastingly binding; and this amounts *thus far at least*, That Judges, Rulers and Magistrates, which are promised under the New Testament, to be given in mercy, and to be of *singular usefulness, as the Judges were under the Old,* are to take care, That the gospel-church, may, *in its concernments as such, be supported and promoted, and the truth propagated,* wherewith they are intrusted.——Know, that ERROR and FALSEHOOD have *no right or title,* either from God or men, *unto any privilege, protection, advantage, liberty, or any good thing,* you are intrusted withal. To dispose that unto a LIE, which is the *right of, and due* to TRUTH, is to *deal treacherously with Him,* by whom you are employed*. Know, that in things of practice, so OF PERSUASION, that are *impious and wicked,* either in themselves or natural consequences, the *plea of conscience is an aggravation of the crime.* If mens *conscience be feared,* and themselves given up to a *reprobate mind,* to do those things, that are not convenient, there is no doubt but they ought to suffer such things as are assigned and appointed by God to 'such practices †." A truly golden speech, and which nothing, but the deepest conviction of its truth, could have drawn from an Independent, in his then circumstances.

Upon the whole, Sir, I readily grant, that a multitude of cavils may be started against the magistrates power about religious matters mentioned in our excellent Standards, as may be against every divine truth, the most fundamental not excepted; and that the proper application of it to practice may be, in some circumstances, not a little difficult. But not cavils however specious; nor difficulty of upright performance of duty, but demonstrative arguments of its sinful-

* P. 52, 53. † P, 54.

ness will warrant my renouncing a principle which I have so solemnly espoused in ordination vows and covenants with God ; and far less to admit, That mens conscience and magistrates ought, in the name of God, to *warrant, encourage*, and *protect* men in *gross heresy, blasphemy* and *idolatry*, though they cannot warrant, encourage, or protect them in doing any civil injury to men. Perhaps, Tindal alone hath raised as many shrewd objections against the divine authority of our Bible, as have, or can be, raised against that power of magistrates mentioned in our Standards ; and yet Wo, wo, wo for ever, to my soul, if, ou that account, I renounce it, as an imposture of Satan.

LETTER II.

On the PERFIDY of all AUTHORITATIVE TOLERATION of *gross Heresy, Blasphemy* or *Idolatry*, in BRITAIN.

SIR,

TO exhibit the contrariety of an *authoritative toleration* of gross heresy, blasphemy, and idolatry, to many, if not all the Burgess Oaths, in our country, and to the established oaths of allegiance to His Majesty, or even to his own Coronation Oath, to maintain the true Protestant religion, as by law established in his dominions, and to our Solemn vows in Baptism and the Lord's Supper, I leave to some fitter hand, and shall only represent it as a violation of these public covenants with God, which our fathers framed, as their strongest human securities against gross heresy, blasphemy, idolatry, Popery, and every thing similar.

Being

Being treacherously and cruelly opposed in their reformation of religion, by their two Popish Queens, the Protestant Lords and others in Scotland, entered into five several bonds, A. D. 1557, 1559, 1560, 1563, in which they solemnly engaged to assist and protect each other, in promoting the free exercise of the Protestant religion. It was only the smaller part of the Protestants in our land, which entered into these bonds,—nor doth it appear, they were intended as general obligations.—But, when the Papists abroad were labouring, with all their might, to extirpate the Protestant religion; and the Pope was found to have granted dispensations for qualifying his votaries, to undermine it in our land,—the *National Covenant* was formed and sworn in 1581—in order to frustrate their attempts, and secure the reformation attained. In it the abominations of Popery were expresly and particularly abjured; and it was understood as adhered to and renewed in every religious bond that followed. After God had marvellously frustrated the attempts of the Spaniards and other Papists against Britain, our fathers, in thankfulness to Him,—and to secure themselves against the Popish confederates abroad, and their friends at home,—with much unanimity and joy renewed their *National Covenant*, A. D. 1590, along with the subscription of a General Bond for preservation of the Protestant religion, and the King's Majesty. In 1596, apprehensions of danger from the Popish Lords, and the treacherous regard shewed them by K. James, and especially a very extraordinary effusion of the Holy Ghost on the General Assembly, issued in much solemn mourning for sin, and renovation of their covenant with God. After forty years of fearful perfidious apostacy, and much sinful veering towards the abjured abominations of Popery, they, awakened by K. Charles and Archbishop Laud's imposition of an almost Popish *Liturgy* and *Book of Canons*,—Searched out, and lamented, their perfidy to God, as the cause of their manifold miseries; and solemnly renewed their covenant with Him, as a mean of obtaining his gracious assistance, and securing their Protestant religion and liberties. Affrighted by the Papists massacring of about two hundred thousand Protestants

Protestants in Ireland, instigated by their distresses in England, and encouraged by the remarkable countenance of God's Spirit and Providence to the Scotch covenanters, Most of the English and Irish Protestants in 1643 and 1644, along with them, entered into a Solemn League and Covenant with God, and with one another, in which they expresly abjured Popery, and Prelacy as a branch of it.—K. Charles had scarce granted a peace, a kind of establishment of their religion to the murderous Papists in Ireland; and Duke Hamilton's attempts to restore him to his throne without giving any security for religion or liberty miscarried in England, when the Scots, and not a few of the Irish renewed their Covenant, with a solemn acknowledgment of sins and engagement to duties.——To manifest the fearful perfidy of all *authoritative toleration* of gross heresy, blasphemy, idolatry, Popery, and every other form of encouragement to, or reception of them, the *solemn*, the *religious* nature of these covenants, and their *extensive* and *perpetual obligation* must be considered.

God alone hath a supreme and unlimited authority and right to regulate his own, and the conduct of all his creatures, Psal. lxxxiii. 18. Dan. iv. 35. James iv. 12. But the very constitution of a rational creature, implies a power derived from him to govern itself, even as mens standing in the relation of parents, masters, magistrates, or church-rulers, necessarily implies their power to govern others,—*in subordination to him*. By virtue of their divinely originated authority over others, parents, masters, and other rulers make laws, or binding rules, for directing the external behaviour of those who are committed to their charge. And by their authority derived from God to *rule their own* Spirit, and to *govern* and *keep in subjection their whole body*, Prov. xvi. 32. James iii. 2. 1 Cor. ix. 27. all men are empowered to make for themselves laws of self engagement, in promises, oaths, vows and covenants, which extend to their purposes and inclinations as well as to their external acts. And, as all the authority, which men have over themselves or others, is derived from that supreme and independent authority, which is in God himself, and is communicated to them, by an act of his will, and is implied in his giving them such a nature and station, it is plain, that no human laws of authority, or self engagement, can have any obligation or binding force, but what are regulated by and subordinated to the divine laws of nature or revelation, 2 Cor. xiii. 8 and that, if such laws and engagements be lawful, God, not only doth, but must necessarily ratify them, his law requiring the fulfilment of them, under pain of his highest displeasure. Rom. xiii. 1,—6. Mat. v. 33.

As no *deputed authority* derived from God, can increase that supreme, that infinite authority, which he hath in himself; so no human command or engagement can increase that infinite obligation to duty, which his law hath *in itself*. But, if lawful, they have in them a *real obligation, distinct,* though neither *separated* nor *separable,* from the obligation of God's law. To pretend with Bellarmine and other Papists, that our promises or vows do not bind us *in moral duties* commanded by the law of God, is manifestly absurd. It necessarily infers, that all human commands of superiors as well as human promises, oaths, vows, and covenants, are in themselves destitute of *all binding force,* except in so far as they relate to such trifling things, as the law of God doth not require of men in such particular truths; and thus saps the foundation of all relative order and mutual trust and confidence among mankind. Commands of superiors must be *mere declarations* of the will of God in his law, and promises, oaths, vows and covenants must be nothing but *mere acknowledgments,* that God's law requires such things from us,—in so far as relating to moral duties. It represents the authority which God hath in himself, and with which he hath invested men, as his deputies, as so inconsistent and mutually destructive of each other, that men cannot be bound to the same thing by both. It represents the law of God as necessarily destructive of the being of an ordinance appointed by itself, to promote the more exact observance of itself,—in so far as that ordinance binds to a conscientious and diligent obedience to it. It is contrary to the common sense of mankind in every age, who have all along considered

dered mens promises, oaths and covenants, as *binding them to pay their just debts*, perform their *just duties* of allegiance or the like, and to declare the truth and nothing but the truth in witness bearing, &c. It is contrary to scripture, which represents promises, promissory oaths, vows, and covenants, as things which are to be *performed, paid*, or *fulfilled*, and which may possibly be *transgressed and broken*, Mat v. 33. Deut. xxviii. 21, 22, 23. Eccl. v. 4. Psal. xxii. 25. & l. 14. & lxi 8. & lxvi. 13. & lxxvi. 11. & cxvi. 13,—18. & cxix. 106. Isa. xix. 21. Judges xi. 35. Isa. xxiv. 5. Jer. xxxiv. 18.—which represents an oath as a strong and decisive *confirmation*, putting an end to all doubt or strife, Heb. vi. 16,—18.—and which in one of the plainest and least figurative chapters of it, repeatedly represents a vow, as constituted by our *binding ourselves, binding our own souls with a bond*, and represents a vow as a *bond* or *obligation*, Heb ISSAR, *a very fast and strait binding bond* or *obligation*,—as our own *bond*, that stands upon or against us, Num. xxx. 2,——12—*Self-binding, self engagements*, is so much the *essential form* of vows, and of all covenants, promises, or promissory oaths, whether of God or man, that they cannot exist at all, or even be conceived of without it, any more than a man without a soul, or an angel without an understanding and will. To represent vowing as a *placing of ourselves more directly under the law of God*, or any command of it; or, as a *placing of ourselves in some new relation to the law*, is but an attempt to render unintelligible that which the Holy Ghost hath, in the above-mentioned chapter, laboured to make plain, if it doth not also import, that we can place ourselves *more directly* under the moral law than God hath or can place us, or, more directly than Christ was placed.—To pretend, that mens commands or engagements derive their whole obligation from the *law of God's requiring* us to *obey* the one,—and *pay, or fulfil* or *perform* the other, is no less absurd.— These divine commands, requiring us to obey, pay, perform or fulfil human laws and engagements, *plainly suppose* an *intrinsic* obligation, in these laws and engagements, and powerfully enforce it. But no law of God can require me to OBEY a human law, or ful-

N

fil an engagement which hath no obligation in itself, any more than the laws of Britain can oblige me to PAY a Bill, or FULFIL a Bond confifting of nothing but mere cyphers.

The *intrinſic obligation* of promiſes, oaths, vows, and covenants which conſtitutes their very eſſence or eſſential form, is totally and manifeſtly diſtinct from the obligation of the law of God in many reſpects. (1.) In his law, God, by the declaration of his will, as our ſupreme Ruler, binds us, Deut. xii. 32. In promiſes, vows, covenants, and promiſſory oaths, we, as his deputy-governors over ourſelves, by a declaration of our will, *bind ourſelves with a bond, bind our ſouls with our own bond, our own vow,* Num. xxx. Pſalm lxvi. 13, 15. & cxix. 106, &c. (2.) The obligation of our promiſes, oaths and covenants is alway ſubject to examination by the ſtandard of God's law, as to both its matter and manner, 1 Theſſ. v. 21. But it would be preſumption, blaſphemous preſumption, to examine, Whether, what we know to be the law of God be right and obligatory, or not, James iv. 11, 12. Iſa. viii. 20. Deut. v. 32. (3.) The law of God neceſſarily binds all men to the *moſt abſolute perfection in holineſs,* be they as incapable of it as they will, Matth. v. 48. 1 Pet. i. 15, 16. No man can, without mocking and tempting of God, bind himſelf by vow or oath to any thing, but what he is able to perform. No man may vow to do any thing which is not in his own power, and for the performance of which he hath no promiſe of ability from God. But, no mere man ſince the fall is able, in this life either in himſelf or by any grace received from God, *perfectly* to keep the commandments of God, Eccl. vii. 20. James iii. 2. While God remains God, his law can demand no leſs than abſolute perfection in holineſs. While his word remains true, no mere man ſince the fall, in this life, can poſſibly attain to it ; and therefore ought never to promiſe or vow it. The leaſt imperfection in holineſs, however involuntary, breaks the law of God, and is even contrary to the duty of our relative ſtations of huſbands, parents, maſters, magiſtrates, miniſters, wives, children, ſervants or people, 1 John iii. 4. Rom. vii. 14, 23, 24. But it is only by that
which

which is, in some respect, *voluntary sinfulness*, that we break our lawful vows, Psal. xliv. 47. Nothing can more clearly mark the distinction of the two obligations, than this particular. There is no evading the force of it, but either by adopting the Arminian *new law* of sincere obedience, or by adopting the Popish perfection of saints in this life. (4.) The law of God binds *all men for ever*, whether in heaven or hell, Psal. iii. 7, 8. No human law or self-engagement binds men, but *only in this life*, in which they remain imperfect, and are encompassed with temptations to seduce them from their duty. In heaven they have no need of such helps to duty, and in hell they cannot be profited by them.

The obligation of lawful promises, oaths, vows and covenants, as well as of human laws, respecting moral duties, however *distinct*, is no more separable from the obligation of God's law, than Christ's *two distinct natures* are separable, the one from the other, but closely connected in manifold respects. In binding ourselves to necessary duties, and to other things so long and so far as is conducive thereto, God's law as the only rule to direct us how to glorify and enjoy him, is made the rule of our engagement. Our vow is no *new rule* of duty, but a *new* bond to make the law of God *our rule*. Even Adam's engagement to perfect obedience in the covenant of works was nothing else. His fallibility in his estate of innocence, made it proper, that he should be bound by his own consent or engagement, as well as by the authority of God. Our imperfection in this life, and the temptations which surround us, make it needful, that we, in like manner, should be bound to the same rule, both by the authority of God, and our own engagements. It is in the law of God, that all our deputed authority to command others, or to bind ourselves is allotted to us. The requirement of moral duties by the law of God obligeth us to use all lawful means to promote the performance of them; and hence requires human laws and self-engagements, and the observance of them as conducive to it. Nay they are also expressly required in his law, as his ordinances for helping and hedging us in to our duty. In making lawful vows, as well as in making human laws, we exert the *deputed authority* of God, *the supreme Lawgiver*, granted to us in his law, in the manner which his law prescribes, and in obedience to its prescription. In forming our vows as an instituted ordinance of God's worship, which he hath required us to receive, observe, and keep pure and entire, Psal. lxxvi 11 & cxix 106. & lvi. 12. Isa. xix. 18, 21. & xlv. 23, 24. & xliv. 5. Jer. l. 5. 2 Cor. viii. 5.—we act precisely according to the direction of his law, and in obedience to his authority in it,—*binding ourselves with a bond, binding our soul with a bond,* Num. xxx. 2,—11.—*binding ourselves by that which we utter with our lips,* ver. 2, 6, 12. —*binding ourselves with a binding oath,—binding ourselves—binding our soul by our own vow—our own bond,* ver. 4, 7, 14. In forming our vow, we, according to the prescription of his own law, solemnly constitute God, who is the supreme Lawgiver and Lord of the conscience,—the witness of our self-engagement, and the Guarantee, graciously to reward our evangelical fulfilment of it, and justly to punish our perfidious violation of it. The more punctual and faithful observation of God's law, notwithstanding our manifold infirmities and temptations, and the more effectual promoting of his glory therein, is the END of our self-engagements, as well as of human laws of authority. And by a due regard to their binding force, as above stated, is this end promoted.—as hereby the obligation of God's law is the more deeply impressed on our minds, and we are shut up to obedience to it, and deterred from transgressing it——In consequence of our formation of our vow, with respect to its matter, manner, and end, as prescribed by God He doth, and necessarily must ratify it in all its awful solemnities, requiring us by his law, to *pay* it as a bond of *debt*, —to *perform* and *fulfill* it as an engagement to duties, and an *obligation* which *stands upon* or *against* us, Num. xxx. 5, 7, 9, 11. with Deut. xxiii. 21.—23 Psalm lxxvi. 11. & l. 14. Eccl. v. 4, 5 Mat. v 33. In obedience to this divine requirement, and considering our vow, in that precise form, in which God in his law, adopts and ratifies it, and requires it to be fulfilled

filled, We pay, perform, and fulfil it *as a bond*, wherewith we, in obedience to Him, *have bound ourselves*, to endeavour universal obedience to his law, as our only rule of faith and manners. Whoever doth not, in his attempts to obey human laws or to fulfil self enagements, consider them as having that binding force which the law of God allows them, he pours contempt on them, as ordinances of God, and on the law of God for allowing them a *binding force*. Thus, through maintaining the *superadded* but *subordinate* obligation of human laws, and of self-engagements to moral duties, we do not make void, but establish the obligation of God's law.

The obligation of a vow, by which we engage ourselves to necessary duties commanded by the law of God, must therefore be INEXPRESSIBLY SOLEMN. Not only are we required by the law of God before our vow was made; but we are bound, in that performance, to fulfil our vow, as an engagement or obligation founded in the supreme authority of his law warranting us to make it. We are bound to fulfil it as a mean *of further impressing* his authority manifested in his law, upon our own consciences,—as a bond securing and promoting a faithful obedience to all his commandments. We are bound to fulfil it, in obedience to that divine authority, by derived power from which, we as governors of ourselves made it to promote his honour. In those or like respects, our fulfilment of our vows is a direct obedience to his whole law.——We are moreover bound to fulfil it, as a solemn ordinance of God's worship, the essential form of which lies in *self obligation*, and must be received, observed, kept pure and entire, and holily and reverently used, and so in obedience to Command I. II. III. We are bound to fulfil it, as an ordinance of God, in which we have *pledged our own truth, sincerity and faithfulness*; and so in obedience to Command IX. I. II. III. We are bound to fulfil it, as a solemn deed or grant, in which we have made over our persons, property, and service to the Lord and his church; and so in obedience to Command I. II. VIII. nay, in obedience to the whole law of love and equity, Mat. xxii. 37, 39. & vii. 12. We are bound to fulfil it
from

from regard to the declarative glory of God, as the witness of our making of it, that he may appear to have been called to attest nothing, but sincerity and truth ; and so in obedience to Command I. III. IX. We are bound to fulfil it from a regard to *truth, honesty,* and *reverence of God,* as things not only commanded by his law, but good in themselves, agreeable to his very nature, and therefore necessarily commanded by him,—and from a detestation of falsehood, injustice, and contempt of God, as things intrinsically evil, contrary to his nature, and therefore necessarily forbidden in his law ; and thus in regard to his authority in his whole law, as necessarily holy, just and good We are bound to fulfil it, from a regard to the holiness, justice, faithfulness, majesty, and other perfections of God, as the Guarantee of it, into whose hand we have committed the determination and execution of its awful sanction,—as the gracious rewarder of our fidelity, or just revenger of our perfidy, —and hence in regard to our own happiness, as concerned in that sanction.——In fine, We are bound to fulfil it in obedience to that command of God, which adopts and ratifies it, requiring us to *pay, fulfil,* or *perform* our vow, oath or covenant, Psal. l. 14. & lxxvi. 11. Eccl. v. 4. Deut. xxiii. 21,—23 Mat. v. 33.

In VIOLATING such a vow, We do not merely transgress the law of God, as requiring the duties engaged, before the vow was made. But we also rebel against, and profane that divine warrant, which we had to make our vow. We profane that authority over ourselves in the exercise of which we made the vow, and consequentially that supreme authority in God, from which ours was derived ; and so strike against the foundation of the whole law. We manifest a contempt of that law, which regulated the matter and manner of our vow. We profane the vow, as an ordinance of God's worship, appointed in his law. By trampling on a noted mean of promoting obedience to all the commands of God, We mark our hatred of them, and prepare ourselves to transgress them, and endeavour to remove the awe of God's authority and terror of his judgments from our consciences. We blasphemously represent the Most High as

a wila willing Witness to our treachery and fraud. We pour contempt on him, as the Guarantee of our engagements, as if he inclined not, or durst not avenge our villainy. Contrary to the truth and faithfulness required in his law, and pledged in our vow, we plunge ourselves into the most criminal deceit and falsehood. Contrary to equity, we rob God and his church of that which we had solemnly devoted to their service. Contrary to devotion, we banish the serious impression of God's adorable perfections Contrary to good neighbourhood, we render ourselves a plague and curse, and encourage others to the most enormous wickedness. Contrary to the design of our creation and preservation, we reject the glory of God, and obedience to his law from being our end. Meanwhile, we trample on the ratification of our vow, by the divine law in all its awful solemnities, and manifold connections with itself,—and requirement to pay it.

It is manifest, that our covenanting ancestors understood their vows in the manner above represented. They never represent them as *mere acknowledgments* of the obligation of God's law, or as placing themselves in *some new relation to God's law*, or *more directly under any command* of it. But declare that a man *binds himself* by a promissory oath to what is good and just.—It cannot oblige to sin; but in any thing not sinful, being taken, it binds to performance.—By a vow *we more strictly bind ourselves to necessary duties* *. And, in expressions almost innumerable, they represent the obligation of their vows as distinct and different, tho' not separable from the law of God †. They no less

⁎ Confess. XXII. 3 4, 6.

† Stevenson's hist. P. 345, 346, 347, 348, 354, 384, 433, &c. Sir James Stewart, afterward advocate to K. William, in *Naphtali*, P. 369. and *Jus populi divinum*, p. 118. Brown in *Apologetical Relation*, p. 341, 363, 364. *Covenanters Plea*, p 9, 10, 68. Durham on commands, p. 14, 121, 122, 129, 130, 131, 132. 135. 137. 138 See also R. Erskine's works, Vol. I. p. 62, 170, 303, 419, 489. Vol. II. p. 109, 141, 224, 227. Discourse at renewing of the Covenants at Lismahago, p. 11. Synod's Catechism on the third command, Q. 49, 50.

plainly

plainly declared, that no man may bind himself by oath to any thing, but what he is ABLE and resolved to perform;—no man may vow any thing which is not in his own power, and for the performance of which he hath no promise of ability from God ‡. And in their several forms of covenant, they never once pretend to engage performing of duties in that *absolute perfection* which is required by the law of God,—but *sincerely, really,* and *constantly,* to ENDEAVOUR the performance of them.

II. These public covenants of our ancestors, in which they abjured the Popish and other abominations, may be called NATIONAL, because the representatives, or the greater or better part of the nation, jointly entered into them, as covenants of duty grafted upon the covenant of grace. But they ought never to be called *national* or *civil*, in order to exclude them from being *church-covenants*, and thus diminish the solemnity or continuance of their obligation. Both church and state jointly promoted them, and in different respects they related to both, being at once covenants of men with God, and with one another. In so far as therein they covenanted with one another, with an *immediate* view to promote or preserve what belonged to the state, they served instead of a civil bond. But at the same time, they covenanted with one another as church-members, in subordination to their covenanting with God himself as their principal party. ——The ratifications given to these covenants by the State were really *civil ratifications*, which adopted them as a part of the laws of the State.—— But that no more rendered them *merely civil* covenants, than the civil ratifications given to, and embodying our Confessions of Faith, made them *merely civil confessions*, and mere acts of Parliament,—or than the repeated legal establishment of our Protestant religion in doctrine, worship, discipline and government, made it a mere *civil religion*. These covenants were sometimes used as means of promoting civil purposes. But that will no more prove them merely civil, than the

‡ Hall on Gospel worship, Vol. II. p. 278, 285.

use of fasting and prayer for advancing or securing the welfare of the State, will prove them a *mere civil worshipping of God.* These covenants were formed for promoting the happiness of both church and state, and were calculated to answer that end. But so is the christian religion and all the ordinances of it, if duly observed, 1 Tim. i. 8. Prov. xiv. 34. I admit, that there was sometimes too mixed an interference of civil and ecclesiastical power in enjoining these covenants. But abuse of things doth not alter their nature. God's ordinances are too often used in a carnal, sensual and devilish manner, without ever being rendered such themselves. It is only, as *really religious covenants,* and not as *civil* or *state covenants,* they can be adopted into ordination vows or baptismal engagements. And that they were such, the following arguments evince.

1. The Covenanters themselves, who best knew their own intentions do, times without number, represent them as VOWS, which their Confession declares to be a *religious ordinance,* as covenants *with God,* which must be *religious,* if any dealings with him be so *. The Assembly in 1649, in their last session, represent them as *confirmations of that right which the Father had given Christ* to the ends of the earth. ——— They, times without number, call them *religious* covenants, —a *religious* covenant *with God,*—among themselves,—a *voluntary* covenanting with God,—a *more free service to God,* than that which is commanded by civil authority; and hence distinguish their covenant, as having a *religious* and *perpetual* obligation, —from acts of parliament establishing religion, which are changeable, and of the nature of a civil ratification †. Concerning the Solemn League, Principal Baillie says, The English were for a *civil* league, we

---

* Chap. XXII. 6. Lar. Cat. Q. 108. Calderwood's Hist. P. 307, 318. Dickson, Henderson and Cant's answers to doctors of Aberdeen, p. 8, 9, 61, 50. Act of Assembly, 1638, p. 21. Supplication of Ass. 1639, to K. Charles. Letter of Ass. 1645, to Dutch.

† Stevenson's history of church of Scotland, P. 343, 347, 349, 350, 348.

for a *religious*. They were brought to us in this ‡. The Assembly 1645, in their Letter to the Dutch, say of it, "Having made a *religious* covenant, even as *bound to God* by the firmest bond, that God might avert his wrath already smoking and hanging over our heads,—a covenant *renewed with God*, (which shews that the Scots considered it as a real *renovation* of their *national covenant*) a *religious* covenant with God and among ourselves.—If it should seem meet to your prudence to think of joining in the *religious fellowship* of such a covenant." How absurd, for persons of weaker capacities and less instructed by the Spirit of God, to pretend, at this distance of time, to know better the nature of their covenants, than themselves did!

2. Except perhaps in 1581, the church, in her General Assemblies, or Commissions, took the lead in promoting the covenanting work. And the state, when it did any thing, did little more than ratify the deeds of the church appointing these covenants to be sworn §. Nay to me it appears evident, that even from 1581 to 1595, the national covenant was subscribed more in obedience to the church, than in obedience to the state.

3. In A. D. 1596 and 1638, in which the covenanting work was *most delightfully* carried on, in Scotland, the state had no influence at all in promoting it. Nay in 1638, the court did all it could, to oppose the covenanters procedure. Indeed our zealous ancestors in the preamble to their bond of that year quote many acts of Parliament in favours of that religion to which they engaged, and of the stedfast maintenance of it. But they never considered these acts as a part of their bond, or as a command to covenant in their manner; but as an evidence that they were doing nothing rebellious or treasonable, as their adversaries

‡ Baillie's Letters, Vol. I. P. 381.

§ Calderwood, P. 220, 248, 254. Act of Ass. 1639, Aug. 30th, with act of convention that day. Act of Commission, Oct. 11th, with act of Commissioners of Estates, Oct. 12th, 1643. and act of Parl. July 15th, 1644. Act of Commission, Oct. 6th, 1648, with act of Committee of Estates, Oct. 14th, and act of Parl. Jan. 5th, 1649.

pretended. Nay, till 1640, no act of Parliament enjoined covenanting work.

4. All along in Scotland, England and Ireland, ministers not statesmen, were the ordinary administrators of these covenants. And upon religious occasions on the Lord's day, before administration of his Supper, or solemn fasting, were they appointed to be taken *. If, without law, laymen sometimes administered them, that will no more prove them *merely state covenants*, than mid-wives baptizing of children, will constitute baptism a *mid-wife ordinance*. To protect them from the insults of Popish and other profane opposers, the ministers in A. D. 1590, had a royal commission, and a number of attendants appointed them, when they administered the covenant. But that will no more prove, that they acted as *civil judges*, than that ministers, receiving an order from King or Parliament to observe a public fast, or hold a Synod, they must, in their fasting and judging work, renounce Christ's sole headship over his church, and adopt the magistrate into his place.—If it is pretended, that ministers marrying of persons is *not a religious* but *civil* work, I insist, that the marriage of Christians, which is to be *only in the Lord*,—to bring up an *holy seed* for Him and his church, and the family to be a *church in the house*, and the parties mutual duty copied from, and influenced by the example of Christ,—and as it is a *covenant of God* which is not like civil contracts, dissolvable by the will of parties, be plainly proven to be a *merely civil* and *nowise religious* bond. If bishops, as spiritual lords, administer the king's coronation-oath, I leave it to others to explain and defend their conduct.—It is certain, the defence of religion is a leading article in that oath.

* Calderwood, P. 248. Stevenson, p. 291, 294. Baillie's Let. Vol. I. p. 45. Livingston's life, p. 22. Wilson's defence, p. 237,---243. Letter of Ass. 1640, to Helvetians. Act of Ass. Oct. 1581. Acts of Ass. Aug. 8th, 17th, and Commission, Oct. 11th, 1643, and of June 3d, 1644, and Aug. 7th, 1648, and of Commission and Committee of Estates, Oct. 6th, 14th, 1648, and of Parl. Jan. 5th, 1649, and of Eng. Parl. Feb. 2d, 9th, 1644.

5. There

5. There appears nothing in the origination of these covenants, which can prove them *merely civil*. Nothing appears in the five bonds of our Reformers, in 1557, 1559, 1560, 1563, but may well accord to the nature of a religious engagement. As Christians, and not merely as civil lords, they bound themselves,—chiefly to promote the true religion according to God's word.——Had K. James been not only the original adviser, but even the framer of the *National Covenant*, it might nevertheless have been a religious bond. The psalms which K. David penned and James versified, are not thereby rendered *merely civil*. The fast which K. Jehoshaphat appointed, and at which he publicly prayed, was *really religious*, not *merely civil*. Our Confessions of Faith and Protestant religion were not rendered *merely civil*, though in 1560 and 1690, the State took the lead in the ratification and establishment before any General Assembly of these periods. It is not improbable, that the ministers of the church had a principal hand in the origination of our national covenant. In 1580, James was about fourteen years of age, and by no transcendent genius, qualified for the work. Just before, and quickly after, we find him marking his hatred of true reformation. His ruling favourites were not a little suspected and complained of, by the zealous clergy, as addicted to Popery.——Through the tearing out of the minutes of four sessions of the Assembly, October 1580, by some parasite of the court, Calderwood's history, at least his printed abridgment, is imperfect on this period. He only says, that " the second Confession of Faith, i. e. *national covenant*, commonly called the King's Confession, was subscribed by the King and his houshold, i. e. *privy council*, January 28th, 158 , which is but an appendix to the First, i e *Scotch Confession*, and comprehends it ; and so both are one,—that a charge was subscribed by the King, March 2d. whereby subjects of all ranks were charged to subscribe the Confession, (national covenant) and requiring ministers to demand said subscription, and to censure such as refused.——The General Assembly in April approved the said Confession, and enjoined the subscription of it.——The Assembly in October peremptorily enjoined

enjoined ministers, to see that this Confession of Faith be subscribed, by all under their charge.——The Assembly in February 1588, enjoined all ministers to deal with noblemen and gentry to subscribe this Confession of Faith.——In March 1590, the privy council, at the earnest desire of the Assembly, appointed about ninety-six ministers to conveen before them, persons of all ranks to subscribe the Confession and general Bond.——The Assembly appointed the Confession and Bond to be subscribed *anew* on copies printed by Robert Waldgrave," (in 4to, and fronted with these scriptures, Josh. xxiv. 15. 2 Kings xi. 17. Isa. xliv. 5. which certainly respect religious covenants) *. Petry affirms, " That Romish dispensations for Papists to swear the oaths, or do other things required of them, providing they continued true to the Pope in their heart,—being shewed to K. James (but whether by ministers appointed to watch over the dangers of the church, he says not) occasioned the formation and swearing of the national covenant, in order to defeat the intention of them. Mr. Craig, a celebrated minister, formed the draught of it at the desire of King James," (and perhaps instigated James to desire it) †.——With respect to James' conduct in the drawing, and first subscription of this covenant, Spotswood, who had the best access to original vouchers, had he been inclined to a faithful use of them, says, " So careful was the King to have the church satisfied and the rumours of the Court's defection from the (Protestant) religion repressed ‡ "——Remarks in Williamson's Sermon, 1703, says, " The Presbyterian party, A. D 1580, got an act of Assembly at Dundee against Episcopacy. That did not content them. They raised mighty jealousies against the King and his court, as if they intended to re-introduce Popery. To convince his subjects of his sincere adherence to the Protestant religion, His Majesty caused his minister John Craig to compile the negative Confession, (national covenant) in the form of an oath. §." Collier says, " This covenant was signed, either by the

* Hist. P. 94, 95, 102, 121, 220, 248, 254.
† Ibid. part 3d, P. 466H   ‡ Hist. p. 308.   § P. 15.

king

king or the lords of the council, at the request of the General Assembly *." Rapin says, " It was drawn up by order of the General Assembly †."

The origination of the Solemn League and Covenant was equally consistent with a *religious vow*. Not a few of the most pious clergymen in England had all along, from Elizabeth's establishment of the Protestant religion, hated part of the ceremonies, and the lordly power of the bishops. Many of these, driven from their charge, by the Prelatical persecution, under Elizabeth and James, and Charles I had been compassionately taken into the families of great men, for the education of their children. Their instruction and example were remarkably blessed, for rendering their pupils and others intelligent and pious. They perceived the encroachments made upon their religion and liberties by Abp. Laud and his assistants, and not a few of them conceived a strong relish for what was then called Puritanism. The success of the Scotch covenanters, in their struggles with the tyrannical court, made many of the English wish and hope for a similar deliverance. In their treaty with Charles 1641, the Scots requested, that the English should be brought to a reformed uniformity with themselves in religion. The Scotch ministers, who attended their Commissioners at London, in forming that treaty of peace, by their instructions and example, recommended their Presbyterian reformation not a little to many of the most learned and pious of the English. A correspondence for promoting a religious uniformity between the two churches was carried on by a number of the English clergymen with the Scotch Assemblies, 1641, 1642, 1643; and by the English parliament with the Assemblies, 1642, 1643. At their request, the Assembly appointed Messrs Henderson, Rutherford, Gillespy and others, to assist the Westminster Assembly in compiling *ecclesiastical Standards*, of doctrine, worship, discipline and government. Alarmed by the terrible massacre of the Protestants in Ireland, and reduced to straits in their war with K. Charles, the English Parliament requested, that for promoting and

* Hist. Vol. II. P. 788. † Hist. Fol. Vol. II. P. 303.

establishing uniformity in religion, and preserving their respective liberties, the two nations might be more closely connected by a mutual League. The Letter from a multitude of English ministers,—the papers from the English parliament and their Commissioners, and the Scotch Assembly's answers, manifest that an uniformity of religion was the principal thing proposed by this League. Henry Vane and perhaps some other English Commissioners, nevertheless, from a dislike of the Scotch Presbyterianism, thought to have gone no further than a *civil* league, but the Scots being positive for a *religious* one, he yielded. It appeared from that readiness and avidity, with which the Solemn League was received in England, that it answered to the wishes of his constituents. After the Westminster Assembly had examined and approved it, the English Parliament appointed it to be sworn by persons of all ranks, and issued forth instructions and an exhortation for promoting that work ‡.

6. There is nothing in the matter of these covenants, which doth not enter into the faith and practice of true religion. They principally engaged to the belief, profession and practice of the true Protestant religion, in doctrine, worship, discipline and government; and renounced, and promised the *regular* extirpation of Popery, Prelacy, and whatever else should, by the word of God, be found contrary to said doctrine, worship, discipline, and government, and holy practice. The preservation of the King's person and authority, and of the rights and privileges of the parliament and nation was promised as a thing subordinated to the interests of religion, in which view, it is a very necessary and important branch of practical Christianity, Rom. xiii. 1,—8. 1 Pet. ii. 13, 17. Tit iii. 1.

7. The manner of covenanting represented in these covenants, corresponds not to *merely civil* but to religious Bonds. In their Bond 1581, 1590, &c. Our ancestors covenanted as *throughly resolved in the truth*

‡ Neal's history of Puritans, Vol. I, II, III. Naphtali, p. 142. Stevenson, Vol. III. Baillie's Let. Vol. I. Acts of Ass. 1642, 1643. Paton's collection of Confessions, p. 58. ———107, 558,——546. Rapin, Vol. II. 481,——484.

by the word and Spirit of God,—as believing it with their heart,—and joining themselves to the reformed kirk in doctrine, faith, religion, and use of the holy sacraments, as lively members of the same, in Christ their Head. If these expressions be but understood, as relating to the visible church, her concerns as such, are of a *spiritual* and *religious* nature, John xviii. 36. Their covenanting in 1596, was so much detached from the State, and so religiously conducted, that you dare not pretend it to have been *state-covenanting:* yet they viewed it as a mere renovation of their national covenant, in a manner suited to their circumstances. Shield in *Hind let loose*, De Foe, Crookshanks, and Stevenson, and Petry in their church-histories, and Gillespy in his *English Popish ceremonies*, call it a renovation of their national covenant *. Epistola Philadelphi subjoined to Altare Damascenum, says, "Their sacred and solemn covenant was renewed, in which men of all ranks covenanted with God, that they would adhere to the religion and discipline †." Calderwood, who was perhaps present, says, "The end of the convention March 1596, was to enter into a new league with God,—hoiding up their hands,—entering into a new league and covenant with God,—that the covenant might be *renewed* in Synods, after the same manner.—The covenant was *renewed* in Synods.—The covenant was *renewed* in Presbytries.—The covenant was *renewed* in Parishes ‡. —In 1604, the whole brethren of the Presbytry of St. Andrews and Synod of Lothian, subscribed the confession of faith and national covenant *anew,* like as they subscribed the same—in the year 1596,—— which confession, i. e. *national covenant* is solemnly *renewed* in the covenant celebrated in the general and provincial Assemblies, Presbytries, and Kirk-sessions, in the year 1596; and how shall any be heard against that which he hath solemnly sworn or subscribed § ? The Assembly 1638, Sef. 17th, say, " The covenant was renewed in 1596." The preamble of the cove-

✤ Hist. on A. D. 1576, English Ceremonies, Part 4. p. 35.
† P. 7.   ‡ Hist. P. 317, 318, 323, 324, 325.
§ Hist. P. 484, 485, 712.

nant,

nant, 1648, affirms, that "the Affembly 1596, and all the kirk judicatures, with the concurrence of the nobility, gentry and burgeffes, did with many tears acknowledge before God the breach of the national covenant, and engaged themfelves to reformation."———In 1638, they covenanted in *obedience to the command of God, conform to the practice of the godly in former times, and according to the laudable example of their worthy and religious progenitors, and of many yet living among them,* (i. e. who had covenanted in 1596.) —They covenanted as *agreeing with their heart to the true religion,—and from the knowledge and confcience of their duty to God,* their king and their country, *without worldly refpect or inducement,* fo far as human infirmity will fuffer ;—*as Chriftians renewing their covenant with God ;—as refolved to be good examples of all goodnefs,* fobernefs and righteoufnefs.—In 1643, they covenanted as *unfeignedly defirous to be humbled for their fins, in not duly receiving Jefus Chrift, and walking worthy of him.*———In 1648, they covenanted in *imitation of their penitent* predeceffors in 1596,—as *deeply affected with their fins, efpecially the undervaluing of the gofpel, that they had not laboured in the power thereof, and received Chrift into their hearts ;—and as really and fincerely penitent ; denying themfelves, and refolving not to lean on carnal confidences, but to lean to the Lord.* Dare you pretend, that all thefe expreffions, in their feveral bonds, reprefent men, *merely as members of a commonwealth,* employed in mere *ftate-covenanting ?*

8. The ends of their covenanting expreffed in their feveral bonds are *religious* not *merely civil.* In 1581 ———1596 and 1604 they covenanted in order to *promote and preferve the profeffion and practice of the true Proteftant religion ;*—in order to *advance the kingdom of Chrift,* as the *principal,* and the welfare of their country as their *fubordinate* end.—In 1638, they covenanted as a *means of obtaining the Lord's fpecial favour,* and of *recovering the purity of religion* ‡. In 1643, they covenanted that *they and their pofterity might* as brethren, *live together in faith and love,* and the *Lord delight to dwell among them ;* and that *the Lord*

‡ Stevenfon's hiftory, P. 284. 351.

might be one, and his name one, in all the three kingdoms, that the *Lord might turn away his wrath and heavy indignation, and establish these churches and kingdoms in truth and peace.*—In 1648 they covenanted, for *advancing the knowledge of God, and holiness and righteousness in the land.*

9. There is nothing in these covenants, or in the seasons of taking them, which doth not perfectly harmonize with a taking hold of God's covenant of grace. Mens belief, profession and practice of the true Protestant religion, and labouring to promote the welfare of their king and country, agree well to it, Tit. ii. 11, 12, 14. & iii. 1, 8, 14. Prov. xxiii. 23. 1 Pet. ii. 13, 17. Rom. xiii. 1,—8, 11,—14.—Their voluntary joining themselves to the church of God as lively members in Christ,—and agreeing with their whole heart to his true religion and ordinances, agree exactly to it, Psal. xxii. 27,—31, & cx. 3. 2 Cor. viii. 5. Having before their eyes the glory of God, and advancement of the kingdom of Christ, and their earnest and constant endeavours, in their stations, that they and their posterity might live in faith and love, delightfully agree with it, Mat. vi. 9, 10. 1 Cor. x. 31. Eph. iii. 14,—19. 2 Thess. iii. 1. Psal. lxxviii. 4,—9. Isa. xxxviii. 19. An unfeigned desire to be humbled for their sin in not duly receiving Christ, and walking worthy of him, and for their unworthy use of the sacraments;—a real and sincere repentance, self-denial, and resolution to lean upon the Lord alone, accord excellently with it, Ezek. xvi. 62, 63. & xxxvi. 25,—32. Phil. iii. 3, 8,—14. The covenanting seasons being remarkable for trouble or danger,—the out pouring of the Holy Ghost,—and deep convictions of sin, are precisely those marked out for that work in scripture, Joel ii. 12, 13. Psal. l. 14, 15. & lxvi. 13, 14. Ezek. xx. 36, 37. Hos. ii, 7, 14. & v. 15. & iii. 4, 5. Isa. xliv. 3,—5. Acts ii. 2 Cor. viii. 5. Jer. l. 4, 5.

These covenants indeed connect fulfilment with gracious rewards, and violation with fearful judgments ‡. But this annexed sanction no more renders them cove-

---

‡ See Covenant-Bonds of 1581, 1638, 1643, 1648.

nants of works, than *so help me God*, in the conclusion of oaths, renders every oath a covenant of works. Notwithstanding this sanction annexed to the Israelites covenants of duty with God, they might well stand stedfast in the covenant of grace, Lev. xxvi. Deut. xxvii,—xxx. 1 Kings ix. In this world, the Law, as a *rule of life*, hath an annexed sanction of gracious rewards and fearful chastisements, as well as it hath as a *covenant*, one of legal rewards and punishments, Psal. i. Isa iii. 10, 11. Exod. xx 6, 12. Rom. ii. 7,—10. & viii. 13. Heb. xi. 6. Gal. vi. 7,—10. 1 Cor. xv. 58. Without Neonomianism, the Holy Ghost calls that which is annexed to believers obedience, a *reward*, and that which is connected with their disobedience, a *punishment*, Psal. xix 11. & lviii. 11. Prov. xi. 18. & xxiii. 18. Mat. v. 12. & x. 41. Gen. xv. 1. Ezra ix. 13. Amos iii. 2. 2 Cor. ii. 6 Lam. iii. 39 Psalm xcix. 8. " The threatenings of God's law shew believers what even their sins deserve, and what afflictions in this world they may expect for them, although freed from the curse thereof, threatened by the law. The promises of it shew them God's approbation of obedience, and what blessings they may expect upon the performance thereof, although not as due to them by the law as a covenant of works; so as a man's doing good, and refraining from evil, because the law encourageth the one and deterreth from the other, is no evidence of his being under the law, and not under grace ‡ "

10 The remarkable effusion of the Spirit of God, which attended the swearing of these covenants, for the conviction, conversion, and confirmation of multitudes, fixing in their hearts such a deep sense of religion, as all the profaneness and persecution of twenty eight years cou'd not eradicate,—is no contemptible evidence that He looked upon them as religious, not merely state covenants. It is at our infinite hazard, if we call that *common and unclean*, which God hath so singularly honoured.

OBJECT. I. " Our Covenanters characterizing themselves *Noblemen, Barons, Burgesses* and *Commons*,

‡ Confess. XIX. 6, 7. Marrow, Part 2d P. 14, 145,—147.

proves their covenants to be *mere civil covenants.*"
Answ. Will then others characterizing themselves *ministers* render them, at the same time, *church-covenants?* Hath Solomon's denominating himself King of Israel, in his Proverbs and Ecclesiastes, rendered these two books merely civil, not religious? If, in a Bond or Bill, I denominate myself *minister of the gospel,* Will that render the Bond or Bill religious and ecclesiastical? (2.) As they never used such characters in their bonds, but when they covenanted contrary to their King's will, they probably intended no more by them, than merely to mark the great harmony of all ranks, for the encouragement of their friends, and the terror of their malicious enemies. (3.) There was no irreligion, in subjecting themselves and all their honours to the service of Jesus Christ, as made of God Head over all things to his Church, Revel. xxi. 24.

Object. II. " In 1638, and 1643, they framed their covenants to admit Episcopalians and Independents, whom they would not have admitted to the sacraments." Answ. As in taking these covenants, men bound themselves to the regular reformation of every thing found sinful, when tried by the word of God, our ancestors agreeable to Rom. xiv. 1. Isaiah xxxv. 3, 4. were willing to help forward the weak, and admit to their covenant and church-fellowship, every person, who appeared willing to receive more light, even though they were not in every respect, equally enlightened and reformed as themselves. But, I defy you to prove, that they excluded one upright covenanter from their religious communion. (2.) The covenants of 1638 and 1643, were not framed to admit any who resolved obstinately to adhere to Episcopacy or Independency. In the bond of 1638, men bound themselves to forbear the practice of Episcopalian government, and of the articles of Perth, till they should be TRIED and ALLOWED in a free General Assembly. The covenanters declare, that their intention in that bond, was against all innovations and corruptions ‡. In the covenant of 1643, that para-

‡ Stevenson's hist. P. 351:

graph, which peculiarly respected the Protestants in England and Ireland was prudently suited to the weakness of many of them. But there is nothing in it, which favours either Episcopacy or Independency. The preservation of the reformation attained in Scotland sworn to, excluded them both. If then Erastians or Independents, and others dissembled with God, and their brethren, in taking it, they, not the covenant, are blameable. Mens hypocritical reception of the sacraments will not render them *civil* ordinances. (3.) You can never prove, that the covenant of 1538 was tendered to the Doctors of Aberdeen, after they had shown their obstinate attachment to Prelacy. Or that Philip Nye, or any others, after manifesting their obstinate attachment to Independency, had the covenant of 1643, tendered to them by any truly zealous covenanter. Baillie affirms, that the Scots were peremptory against keeping open a door to Independency in England ‡.

OBJECT. III. "The imposition of these covenants under civil penalties, proves them to have been merely state covenants." ANSW. No more than the requirement of men under civil penalties, to partake, at least once a year, of the Lord's Supper, rendered it a merely civil ordinance. An ordinance may remain *religious*, though a civil sanction should be sinfully annexed to it. (2.) If, which I do not, you believe, that Asa and Josiah, by penal laws, compelled men to take their covenants, you can scarce condemn our covenanters annexing civil penalties to the refusal of their bonds, especially as they knew, it would scarce come from any, but such as were malignant enemies to the civil as well as religious liberties of the nation. (3.) In 1596, 1638, 1648, and 1649, these covenants had no penalty either civil or ecclesiastical annexed to the not swearing of them, without any hint from the covenanters, that this altered the nature of the engagement.

OBJECT. IV. "Our ancestors gave up with their covenanting work, whenever they got the state of the

‡ Committee of Westminster Ass. answers to Independents, p. 106,--112. Wilsons defence, p. 304. Bail. let. Vol. I. p. 301.

nation settled by means of it; and having got their civil liberties otherwise secured at the Revolution, they never covenanted at all." Answ. (1.) Did ten years of murderous invasion and outrageous contention, and twenty eight years of horrible profaneness and persecution make our nation so happy, that covenanting with God our deliverer was no more necessary? Or, Have the fearful profanation of the name of God by unnecessary and wicked oaths, or the shocking bribery and perjury, too common in the election of our Representatives in Parliament, and our other outrageous abominations, rendered Britain so holy, that these covenants need no more be regarded? (2.) Not the alteration of the national affairs to the better, but the alteration of mens hearts to the worse, made covenanting with God to be so contemned at the Restoration and Revolution.

III. That these *solemn* and *religious* covenants with God, in which all gross heresy, blasphemy, idolatry, Popery, and other abominations have been repeatedly abjured, bind not only the immediate swearers or subscribers, but *all their posterity and other representees, in all generations following, to a faithful performance of every thing engaged*, must now be demonstrated.

1. That which is engaged in these covenants, being moral duty, commanded by the law of God, is of *perpetual obligation*. The whole faith and practice to which we therein engage are stated from the oracles of God, in our excellent Standards. If the matter in itself, were contrary to God's law, no human covenant could bind us, or any represented by us, to it for a moment. We can have no power from God to bind ourselves or others to any thing sinful, 2 Cor. xiii. 8. Nor can any human deed be valid in opposition to his supreme authority.——If the matter were indifferent, no vow or promissory oath could lawfully constitute a *perpetual obligation*, as the alteration of circumstances might render it very unexpedient and unedifying, 1 Cor. vi. 12. & x. 23. & xvi. 14 Rom. xiv. 19. But if that which is engaged, be precisely, what every person, in every age or circumstance, is

bound

bound to, by the antecedent tie of the law of God, no man can be, in the least, abridged of any lawful liberty, by being brought under the most solemn obligation of an oath or vow.——The strictest fulfilment of it cannot but tend to the real profit of every one concerned, both in his personal and his social capacity, Psal. xix. 11. 1 Cor. xv. 58. Isa iii. 10. Proverbs xiv. 34. Rom. ii. 1,—10. It is therefore for the advantage of us and our posterity, to be hedged in, and bound up to the most exact conformity to God's law, by every mean which he requires or allows, in his word,—even as it is for our advantage to have our liberty bounded by the ledges of bridges.——The law of God requires us to do every thing which is calculated to promote or secure our own or our children's walking in the truth, Gen. xvii. 7. Psal. xlv. 17. & lxxviii 1,—9 Isa. xxxviii. 19 3 John, ver. 4.—It represents solemn vows as a mean most effectual to answer this purpose, Psal. cxix. 106. & lxxvi. 11. & l, 14. & lvi 12. & lxvi. 13, 14 & lxi. 8. & cxvi. 12, —19. & cxxxii. 1,—5. Gen. xxviii. 20. Deut, v. 2. & xxix. Josh xxiv. 15, 24, 25. 2 Chron. xv. 12. & xxiii. 16, 17. & xxix. 10. & xxxiv. 30,—32. Ezra x 3. Neh. ix. x. Isa. xix. 18, 21. & xliv. 3,—5. & xlv. 23, 24. Jer. l. 4, 5. 2 Cor. viii. 5.

2. By the repeated judicial acts of both church and state, approving and imposing these covenants, they were constituted the *adopted laws* of both, proper to be acknowledged and submitted to, by all their members, in the most solemn manner, which their circumstances permitted.——Several of these acts, as well as the best duties of Christians, had their sinful infirmities particularly on the head of penalties, which I mean not to defend. But in so far as these acts approved and authorized these covenants, which bound men to receive and hold fast such temporal and spiritual privileges, as God had given them, and thankfully improve them to his glory,—and required a Christian, regular, and seasonable taking of them,—they were certainly good and valid. Being good in themselves, and the exact performance of them calculated to promote the glory of God, and eminent welfare of both church and state, these covenants, if once regularly

adopted

adopted as laws, muſt remain obligatory upon the adopting ſocieties, while they exiſt Civil rulers being ordained *miniſters of God for good* to men, Rom. xiii. 1,—4. and church officers appointed by Chriſt for the *edifying of his body*, Eph. iv. 11,—14. have no power againſt the truth, but for the truth, 2 Corinth. xiii. 8, 10. and ſo can no more repeal a law, which promotes only that which is morally good, any more than they can give validity to a ſinful one.——Theſe covenants muſt therefore, in the view of God and conſcience, continue binding, as laws divinely ratified, upon us, as ſubjects, and as Chriſtians. But it is their much more ſolemn obligation as *public Vows* and *Covenants with God*, which I mean to eſtabliſh, particularly with reference to Scotland.

3. The matter of theſe vows being morally good, calculated to promote the holineſs and happineſs of every perſon in every age, the immediate covenanters were ſuch as laid every poſſible foundation of tranſmitting the obligation of their vow to the whole church and nation, to all generations. The REPRESENTATIVES of both church and ſtate,—the MAJORITY of the Society, and our own PARENTS, in their reſpective ſtations, took theſe covenants. What could tranſmit and extend an obligation to poſterity, if all this did not? You cannot but allow, that even in private civil deeds, the obligation is extended far beyond the *immediate engagers*. In bonds, reſpecting money or ſervice, men bind not only themſelves, but their ſucceſſors, and aſſigns, eſpecially, if they have the continued right to, or poſſeſſion of that fund or property from which that money or ſervice natively ariſeth. The obligations contained in a call to a miniſter, fix on the whole congregation, if ſubſcribed by the majority, without any regular diſſent,—and on ſuch as afterwards accede to it. The treaties of peace, traffick, &c. contracted by Kings, Parliaments, Magiſtrates, are held binding on their ſubjects, and even on their poſterity. They, who accede to any ſociety, fall under the binding force of its ſocial engagements for debt, duty, &c. If bonds and covenants did only bind immediate contractors, nothing but the wildeſt diſorder would enſue. If the immediate engagers, quickly

quickly after died, they who trusted to their engagement, might be totally ruined.—A minority, who had been silent during the transaction, might, in a few days, overturn a bond or contract of the majority. Subjects might, at their pleasure, render void the contracts and treaties of their rulers. To pretend, that men may not use the same freedom, in binding their representees and posterity to God, as in binding them to men, is highly absurd and shocking, as it represents God as more dangerous, and less honourable and useful to be dealt with, than the very worst of men. Why may not a parent, in offering his child to God in baptism, take hold of God to be his God, and the God of his seed after him to all generations, —and dedicate not only that child, but all his posterity to God, as his honoured vassals and servants, Gen xvii. 7. Acts ii. 39 ?—Is this less dutiful, safe, or honourable, than to infeft himself and them in some earthly property, and bind them as possessors of it, to be the vassals of some sinful superior?—If the majority of a society, especially in distress, may put the whole under the authority and protection of a man who is a great sinner, why must they act either wickedly or foolishly, if, by a solemn dedication, they put it under the especial care and protection of the Great GOD our Saviour ? Rev. xi. 15. Psal. ii. 12. & xxii. 27. If the representatives of a people, may bind them to live peaceably and trade honestly with earthly neighbours ; or may, in some cases, subject them to the power, laws, or exactions of other earthly superiors,—why allow them no power to study peace with God, and to follow peace with all men and holiness ?—No power to surrender them to God, to be ruled by his law,—and to render him his due revenues of honour ?—Hath not God an original and supreme right to all men as his creatures, subjects, and children ? Are they not all bound by his law to the whole of that duty, to which, we contend, any man ought to be bound by a vow of *perpetual obligation* ? Is it not inexpressibly honourable, safe and profitable to stand under the special care of, and in relation to God in Christ, Deut. iv. 7. & xxxii. 29, ?

Q Why

Why then more shy of devoting posterity, or other representees to him, than to a sinful man and his service?

In covenants with men, a proper and timely dissent may frequently be well founded; and may effectually divert this obligation from the dissenters. But how there could be a lawful dissent from an engagement carefully to keep all the commandments of God and nothing else, I know not. Had the whole, or even the body of the Hebrew nation, timely and regularly dissented from the treaty made by their princes with the Gibeonites, it might have diverted its obligation from them.—Instead of this, they appear to have agreed to the final stating of it, without a single murmur, Josh. ix. But, if these princes had, by covenant, devoted themselves and their tribes to a careful keeping of God's commandments, I know not how the people's dissent could have diverted the obligation from themselves.——In covenants with men, the non-fulfilment of some condition or some dispensation or remission may weaken, if not perfectly annul, the obligation. But none can dispense with, or grant remissions, in the matters of God. Covenants made with God are more absolute, and less clogged with conditions, and so *more obliging*. The covenants of which we now treat, being about indispensible duties of morality, upon which dependeth the glory of God, the advancement of the kingdom of Jesus Christ, the honour and happiness of magistrates, and the public liberty, safety and peace of the nation, and the good of posterity in all time coming, ought to have their obligation allowed to fix, wherever any ground can be found, while Christ hath a kingdom, and the covenanters a posterity, particularly in Scotland; for,

(1.) Our civil Representatives by these covenants devoted themselves in their station, and their subjects, in so far as under their power, to the service of God. In 1581 and 1590, King James and his privy council took the *National Covenant*, and required their subjects to follow their example. In 1638, the privy council again took it, as it stood in 1581. In 1640, the members of Parliament took it, as explained by the Assembly 1638, to abjure *Prelacy* and the *five articles*

ticles *of Perth*, and appointed it to be sworn by all the members of every future Parliament. It was sworn by the members of Parliament 1644. In 1649, the national covenant, and the Solemn League which was materially the same, were renewed by the members of Parliament, with solemn fasting and humiliation. The oath framed in 1641, to be sworn by members of Parliament, at taking their seats, expresly approved the national covenant. King Charles I. gave a solemn approbation of it. King Charles II. and other magistrates took the covenants in 1650 and 1651. Now, if a covenant made by the princes of Israel with the representatives of the Gibeonites, in a matter which concerned the *Lord's land* and the *remote service of his altar*, extended its obligation to the whole nation of Israel, who consented to it, no otherwise, than by silence at the final stating of it,—and to their posterity, for many generations,—that four hundred years after, they were punished with a famine on account of Saul's breach of it, Josh. ix. with 2 Sam. xxi. and to the Gibeonites and their posterity ;—Why not allow the covenanting deed of our Princes to extend its obligation in like manner ? If magistrates be the *ministers of God for good* to men, Why should they not be capable to surrender themselves and their subjects to the special care and service of God, their common and beneficent Superior ? If they possess the powers assigned them in our excellent Standards, Why may they not, as *nursing fathers* of the church, devote themselves and their subjects of the same true religion, to the enjoyment of God himself in his oracles and ordinances, and to serve Him regularly in Christ ? If Joshua could bind himself and his family to serve the Lord, why may not magistrates bind themselves and their subjects of the same true religion, to receive and hold fast the like honour and happiness ? If for the benefit of their subjects, magistrates may, in a time of need, subject themselves and their people to some powerful Monarch, whose fury is terrible, but his favour extremely profitable, or may approve and ratify some former grant of that kind,---Why may they not for the same end, devote themselves and subjects to the Great GOD our Saviour, and Prince of the kings

of

of the earth? Why may they not bring their glory into the church? and as judges kiss the Son of God, solemnly approving and in their station ratifying that grant which his Father made to him, of the outermost ends of the earth? Rev. xxi. 24. & xi. 15. Prov. viii. 15, 16, Psal. ii. 8,—12.

(2.) In these covenants our Representatives in the church, in their station, devoted themselves and their people to the faith, profession and obedience of Christ, In April 1581, the General Assembly unanimously approved the *national covenant*, and then in October ensuing, in the name of Christ, appointed it to be subscribed by all Protestants. In 1588 and 1590, they made further acts for promoting this subscription. The general Assemblies of 1596, 1638, 1639, and the Commissions or Assemblies of 1643, 1644, 1648, 1649, enjoined the swearing of the covenant by all adult church-members. I do not know of one Presbyterian minister or ruling elder in Scotland, who, in any of the covenanting periods of 1581, 1590, 1596, 1638, 1643, 1648, declined taking it. Now, it civil representatives may bind their subjects and their posterity by civil contracts, Why ought not the harmonious dedication of themselves and people to God, by church-rulers to have a like binding force? If, in public prayers, ministers may devote themselves and congregations to Christ, why may not they and ruling elders conjunctly do it, by public covenant? But we do not chiefly rest the matter on these grounds; for,

(3.) It is beyond all contradiction, that the lawful and public covenants civil or religious, which are made by parents, do bind their posterity. The oath of Esau, in which he resigned his birthright to Jacob, bound his posterity never to attempt recovering the privileges of it, from Jacob or his descendents. Hence Esau and his family, after the death of Isaac, removed intirely from Canaan, Gen. xxv. 33. & xxxvi. 6. Even the public curse, which the Jews took upon themselves and their children, hath been manifestly binding on them these seventeen hundred years past, Mat. xxvii 25. The vow of parents in the antient circumcision, or the Christian baptism of their infants, extends

extends to these children,—nay according to the extent of God's covenant and promise to all their future seed, Gen. xvii. 7. Acts ii. 38, 39. Hence, whatever any of them do contrary to that vow, must at once be perfidy and rebellion against God. Nor will their wilful or slothful ignorance of that obligation, or their non-consent to it, when grown up, free them from that guilt, any more than ignorance of Adam's covenant, or of the breach of it, can free his posterity from the guilt of his first sin, or from perfidy in their personal violations of that covenant of works. In Deut. v. 2, 3. God, by Moses declares, that the covenant made with the Israelites at Sinai, was not made with them only, but with all that new generation of their children and grand children, who survived them, Num. xxvi. 64.—In Deut. xxix. 14, 15. he declares, that the covenant taken by that new generation in the plains of Moab, did not only bind them who were alive and present at the entrance into it, but also others, even their posterity.—Their covenant with the Gibeonites did not only bind the immediate engagers and consenters, but also their posterity, many ages afterward, Josh. ix. 15, 19. with 2 Sam. xxi. 1.——Now, these covenants of allegiance to God and duty to men, of which we are treating, were sworn and subscribed by our own *natural*, tho' now *mediate* parents, and when it is considered, how FREQUENTLY that covenant, the same in substance in the several Bonds, was sworn or subscribed, and how GENERALLY;—and how readily some covenanted on one occasion, whose ancestors had not on a preceding;—and how families have been since intermixed, it will scarce remain probable, that there is a Scotchman, at least on the continent of Britain or Ireland, who is not descended from some covenanter. If any, to his own disgrace, will contend that in all these and different periods of covenanting 1581, 1590, 1596, 1638, 1639, 1643, 1648, &c. all his progenitors were such mere neutrals, or malignant opposers of the true religion and liberties of the country, that none of them took the covenant, let him take heed, lest, after all, God his Creditor find him a perjured transgressor of the covenant of his fathers,—or at least, of the covenant made by his church and nation, and their respective Representatives.

(4.) That lawful covenants, made by the greater part of a society bind the whole, and every future acceder to it,—at least, unless the minority or acceders have, by a proper dissent, diverted the obligation from themselves;—and that, if remarkably calculated to promote the common advantage, they bind the members of it, while it continues a society,—Common sense will not allow us to doubt. That the exact fulfilment of our covenants with God, is remarkably calculated to promote the honour of Christ and his Father, and the welfare of both church and state, hath been formerly hinted. No person therefore could, or can, by any lawful dissent, divert their binding force from himself. Nor do I remember of any, who regularly attempted it in Scotland.

Without doubt, the majority, nay body of the Scotch nation nation entered into their Solemn Covenant with God. In 1581, both the privy council and the General Assembly, in their respective acts enjoined the taking of the National Covenant. "In this year, in the month of March, was the National Covenant solemnly taken by the king, his council and court, and afterwards by the inhabitants of the kingdom [*]." "The National Covenant (was) subscribed by the King, his court, and council, and afterwards by all ranks of people in the land [†]." "That good order of the church was three years ago approved, sealed, and confirmed with profession of mouth, subscription of hand, and religion of oath, by the King, and every subject of every estate [‡]."——"In 1590, the National Covenant was again subscribed by all sorts of persons [§]." "In March 1590, the bond for religion was again ratified in council and about ninety-six ministers, in different parts of the kingdom, were appoint-

---

[*] Brown's *Apologetical Relation*, P. 17.

[†] Crookshank's hist. P. 10.   Comp. Calderwood, p. 96, 101, 121. Spotswood, p. 309. Petry, part 3d, p. 407. Collier, Vol. II. p. 572.

[‡] And. Malvin, in Petry, p. 445.   Comp. Vindiciæ epistolæ Philadelphi, P. 55.   [§] Crookshanks, P. 11.

ed

ed to conveen before them the godly of all ranks, and minister unto them the National Covenant, and to take their subscriptions; and an hundred and thirty of the nobility and gentry to assist them, as should be necessary——In consequence hereof, copies of the covenant and general Bond were dispersed through the whole kingdom, and the covenant subscribed *." " Their Confession of Faith and Solemn League and Covenant (was) subscribed by the whole Scotch nation †." " It was subscribed by all sorts of persons, the whole land rejoicing at the oath of God. It was attended by many choice blessings from the Lord ‡." About this time the General Assembly appointed this covenant to be renewed in Universities every year.— In 1596, the covenant was renewed in the General Assembly by about four hundred ministers, besides elders and others, with great solemnity, and attended by a remarkable effusion of the Holy Ghost, and bitter mourning for sin, and earnest reformation from it. It was afterwards renewed in Synods, Presbytries, and Parishes; but in many parishes, particularly in Edinburgh, where the court had much influence, it was delayed and neglected. In 1604, the covenant was subscribed by all the members in the Presbytery of St. Andrews and Synod of Lothian §.

The renovation of the covenant in 1638, was still more universal and harmonious. " This covenant like an alarm bell brought together all the Scots, who were dissatisfied with the government, that is almost the whole nation. It was subscribed by the great men and the people, except the privy counsellors, the judges, and the bishops, and such ministers as were dig-

---

* Calderwood, P. 248,——254.

† Neal's history of Puritans, Vol. II. P. 259.

‡ Testimony by Rutherford, Guthrie, and 15 other Protestors, p. 14. Comp. Epist. Philadelphi, p. 6. Stevenson's Introduction, p. 164. Willison's Testim. p. 5. Seced. Testimony, p. 17.

§ Calderwood, P. 311, 312, 317, 318, 323, 324, 325, 484, 485, 712. De Foe, p. 132. Crookshanks, p. 13. Brown's Apol. Relat, p. 24, 403. Petry, p. 511, 570. Spotfwood, p. 416. Stevenson, p. 169,---172. Epist. Philad. p. 7. Acts of Ass. 1638. p. 38. Preamble to Covenant 1638 & 1648.

nitaries

nitaries in the church.—By the publication of this covenant, the Royalists were not above one to a thousand. The covenant was the sole law the people would follow, with respect to religion ‡‡." "All ranks and conditions, all ages and sexes flocked to the subscription of this covenant. Few in their judgment disapproved it, and still fewer dared openly to condemn it. The King's ministers and counsellors were, most of them, seized by the general contagion —The covenanters found themselves seconded by the zeal of the whole nation *." "In the several counties and shires, it was received by the common people as a sacred oracle, and subscribed by all such, as were thought to have any zeal for the Protestant religion, and the liberties of their country. The privy counsellors, the judges, the bishops and the friends of arbitrary power were the principal who refused it †." "These rightly judging that the procuring cause of all the calamities of the nation was the violation of their National Covenant, unanimously resolved to renew the same. The town of Aberdeen was the only place of any note in the kingdom, that declined joining in the covenant, ——(yet even there) severals of special note cheerfully put their hands to the covenant, which was sworn by the generality of all ranks through the nation, before the end of April ‡." "They resolved upon renewing the national covenant, which had been almost buried for forty years before.—Being read in churches, it was heartily embraced, sworn, and subscribed by all ranks, with many tears and great joy; so that the whole land great and small, *a very few excepted*, without any compulsion from church or state, did, in a few months cheerfully return to their antient principles, and subject themselves to the oath of God for reformation. Both the court and prelates were enraged against them for it; but the Lord remarkably countenanced them with the extraordinary manifestation of his presence and down-pouring of his Spirit §."

‡‡ Rapin, Vol. II. P. 303.   * D. Hume's hist. on 1638.
† Neal's history of Pu. Vol. II. p. 260.   ‡ Crookshanks, Vol. I. p. 28.   § Willison's Testimony, P. 7.

" The

" The whole body of the people of Scotland were engaged to God, by folemn covenants and vows frequently renewed, to own and endeavour the prefervation of the reformed religion, &c.—Not only did the body of the commonalty, fwear thefe covenants, but the magiftrates themfelves did take on the fame vows and engagements, folemnly promifed to profecute the ends of this covenant. All the lovers of God and friends to the liberties of the nation did folemnly renew the national covenant, wherein they were fignally countenanced of the Lord *." So much for the teftimony of foes and friends, who lived at fome diftance of time.

Let us now hear eye and ear witneffes of that work. " Upon the firft of March 1638, the covenant was publicly read and fubfcribed by them all, with much joy and fhouting —Afterward the covenant was fubfcribed every where in parifhes, with joy, except in the North †." " Within not many months, almoft the whole land did fubject themfelves to the oath of God, which was attended with more than ordinary influences of the Spirit ‡." " The Lord did let forth much of his Spirit on his people, in 1638, when this nation did folemnly enter into covenant.—Then did the nation vifibly own the Lord, and was vifibly owned by him. A remarkable gale of Providence did attend the actings of his people, which did aftonifh their adverfaries, and force many of them to own fubjection §." " Except one day at the kirk of Shots, I never faw fuch motions from the Spirit of God,—all the people *generally* and *moft willingly* concurring (in fwearing the covenant) thro' the whole land, except the profeffed Papifts, and fome few who for bafe ends, adhered to the prelates, the people *univerfally* entered into the co-

---

* Sir James Stewart in Jus Populi, P. 3, 4. He and Stirling in Naphtali, p. 140. Wilfon's defence, p. 236,---243. Stevenfon, p. 291. &c. E q; Guthrie's hift. of Scotland, Vol. IX. p. 238. Burnet's memoirs of the Dukes of Hamilton, on 1638.

† Bifhop Guthrie's memoirs, p. 30.

‡ Teft. by Rutherford, &c. p. 16.

§ Fleming's fulfilling of the fcriptures, p. 401.

nant of God ‡‡." When the covenanting work of that year was still unfinished, Dickson, Henderson, and Cant affirm, that *almost the whole kirk and kingdom had joined in the late covenant*, and that they had been sent to Aberdeen from almost the whole kirk and kingdom. And this the Prelatic Doctors there, grant to be true *. " The covenant being drawn up, was subscribed by all present (at Edinburgh) and copies thereof sent to such as were absent, and being read in the churches, it was heartily embraced, sworn and subscribed, with tears and joy. Great was that day of the Lord's power; for much willingness and cheerfulness was among the people, so as in a short time, few, in all the land did refuse, except some Papists, some aspiring courtiers, some who were addicted to the English ceremonies, and some few, who had sworn the oath (of supremacy and canonical obedience) at their entry ‡." " This covenant was subscribed by almost every assertor of liberty, who was present (at Edinburgh). Copies of it were sent to such as were absent, to be communicated to all the inhabitants of the kingdom, that every one who had religion at heart, might swear this covenant.——The non-covenanters were first all the Papists, the number of whom scarce exceeded six hundred,—some court parasites, who had lately been advanced to dignities, or eagerly grasped at them, or who were more addicted to the English rites and canons,—as the doctors and magistrates of Aberdeen.——Some others for a time declined subscribing from a regard to the oath (of Supremacy and Canonical obedience) which they had taken, and because the king had not enjoined this covenant, and because it bound them to assist one another in this cause §." " The national covenant having been agreed to, with so great harmony, amidst a world of difficulties,—upon the first of March was subscribed by several thousands, consisting of all the nobles, who were then in Scotland, (except the Lords of privy council, and four or five more)—and of commissio-

‡‡ Livingston's life, p. 22.   * Answers to doctors of Aberdeen p. 440.   ‡ Brown's Apol. Relat. p. 48.
§ Spang and Baillie in Historia Motuum, p. 60.

ners from all the Shires within Scotland, and from every Burgh, except Aberdeen, St. Andrews, and Crail,---and of other gentlemen and ministers ———Before the end of April, every parish through Scotland, where the minister was friendly to the reformation then sought, having observed a fast, to humble themselves for the former defection and breach of covenant, did renew the same with great solemnity, *scarce a person* opposing himself, but every one, women as well as men, concurring, and publicly avouching the Lord to be THEIR God, with their right hand lifted up, except, (1.) Papists, to whom it was not offered,---the number of whom in all Scotland, was not reckoned above 600 persons. (2.) Courtiers, who had no will to displease the king. (3.) Some of the clergy, who had sworn the oath for conformity, (to Prelacy) or were dignitaries in the church, the chief of whom were the doctors of Aberdeen.———The most of the Hamiltons, Douglasses, all the Gordons who were under the influence of Sutherland and Kenmure,--all the Campbells, Forbeses, Frasers, Grants, M'Kenzies, M'Kays, M'Intoshes, M'Leans, M'Donalds, Irvines, and Innesses, subscribed the covenant. Many in Aberdeen and Glasgow, who for a time refused, subscribed. Not a burgess in St. Andrews refused ———In Edinburgh Dr. Elliot a minister, and Robert Rankin, and John Brown, Regents of the college, were the only persons of note, who declined subscription *." Add to all these, the 28,000, who, at King Charles's command, subscribed the covenant as it stood in 1581, declared to be the same in substance with the other Bond,---and it will appear that few, very few, then neglected to swear or subscribe the covenant ‡. What numbers took the covenant from 1639 to 1643, in obedience to the peremptory acts of church and state enjoining it, I know not

In 1643 and 1644, the swearing of the *Solemn League and Covenant* by all adult persons, was very peremp-

---

* Stevenson's hist. P. 291, 294, 311. from Baillie's MSS Letters, p. 196,--223. Bail. printed let. Vol. I. p. 45,---49, 66, 73. Acts of the Ass. 1638. p. 14,---41. Stevenson, p. 416. - 418, &c. Large Declaration. Burnet's memoirs of D. Hamilton.

torily required by both church and state. From a copy of it before me, I have reason to think, that the subscription of it was pretty universal The takers of it in Scotland are affirmed to have been seven to one of their opposers ‡. "It was solemnly sworn and subscribed almost in all parts of the nation §." "With a marvellous unanimity was this every where received. In God's great mercy all that I have yet heard of, have taken this oath. Our land now, I hope, in a happy time, hath entered into a league with England ++." In their speech to the council of London, after their return, Henry Vane and Stephen Marshal affirm, That they believed the Solemn League had been *universally* taken by the whole Scotch nation. The exhortation of the English Assembly and Parliament affirms, that the "whole body of Scotland had willingly sworn it, with rejoicing." Rutherford, and his sixteen faithful brethren, affirm, that "the Solemn league was actually sworn and taken by the whole body of Scotland, from the highest to the lowest--- by the whole body of the land +." Sir James Stewart and Mr. Stirling who, perhaps, both covenanted that year, affirm, that "in 1648, in the month of December, (the Solemn League) was, for the second time, sworn in *all the congregations* of Scotland, upon the same day, except where a vacancy, or the minister's being under scandal, did occasion a delay till another day, --with great solemnity and such mixture of joy and sorrow, as became people entering into covenant with the Lord.—There was at that time a great zeal for God, from clear knowledge and sad experience, generally and solemnly professed before God and all men, in our public *acknowledgments* 1648,— in consequence whereof, the League and Covenant was also, by the whole kingdom, renewed that same year, and in answer thereto, the Lord did mightily save us.—He did highly advance his blessed work *."

That the body of the English nation also swore the Solemn League and Covenant, is manifest. The

‡ Stevens, Vol. III.   § Crook. p. 33. Hind let loose p. 80
++ Bail. Let. Vol. I. p. 239, 393.   + Test. p. 20, &c.
* Naphtali, p. 91, 156.

West·

Westminster Assembly and English Parliament, affirm, "The honourable houses of Parliament, the Assembly of Divines, the renowned city of London, and multitudes of other persons of all ranks and quality in this nation, and the whole body of Scotland, have all sworn it, rejoicing at the oath so graciously seconded from heaven. God will, doubtless, stand by all those, who with singleness of heart shall now enter into an everlasting covenant with the Lord §." Rutherford and his sixteen faithful brethren, affirm, that "this Solemn League was actually sworn and taken by the whole body of Scotland,—also by the honourable houses of the parliament of England, the Assembly of Divines, the renowned city of London, and multitudes not only of the people, but of persons of eminent rank and quality throughout that nation, and the nation of Ireland, and all this by the authority of the powers, civil and ecclesiastic. Who can have forgot, how deliberately it was resolved, and how unanimously it was concluded? The respective authorities of both church and state in Scotland, did all with one voice approve and embrace the same, as the most powerful mean by the blessing of God for settling and preserving the true Protestant religion, with perfect peace in these nations, and propagating the same to other nations, did ordain it to be, with *humiliation and all religious* solemnities, received, sworn and subscribed by all ministers and professors within this kirk, and subjects within this kingdom,—which was accordingly done by the whole body of the land, and in many congregations attended with the feelings of that joy, and comfortable influence of the Spirit of God,—which they did find in so great a measure upon the renovation of the national covenant in 1638.——And this solemn oath of God being taken by the honourable houses of the Parliament of England, by the renowned city of London, by the reverend Assembly of Divines,—the Lords and Commons, upon the account of its being thought a fit and excellent means to acquire the favour of God towards the three kingdoms of England, Scotland and Ireland, and to establish

§ Exhortation to take the Covenant, FEBRUARY 1644.

and propagate the true reformed religion, peace and prosperity of these kingdoms, did—ordain, that the same covenant be solemnly taken throughout the kingdom of England. And upon these grounds, and according to these instructions and exhortations of the Assembly and Parliament, was that solemn covenant taken by multitudes of all ranks and sorts, many of which did rejoice at the oath of God. A little thereafter, it was ordered by the House of Commons, that the Solemn League and Covenant be, on every day of humiliation, (*i. e.* once every month) publicly read in every church and congregation, within the kingdom; and that every congregation have one of the said covenants fairly printed on a fair letter, in a table to hang up in some place of the church, to be read, (where many copies continued hanging till the restoration)——No power on earth can absolve either themselves or others from the bond and tie of this sacred oath of the Most High *." An apologetical declaration of the conscientious Presbyterians of the province of London, and of *many thousands* of other faithful and *covenant-keeping* citizens and inhabitants, which was subscribed by these *many thousands* in January, 1649, at the hazard of every thing dear to them, hath these words, " calling to mind our Solemn League and Covenant, which was so *religiously* and *unanimously* sworn †." " The sacred oath was first taken by the Lords and Commons legally assembled in Parliament, then by the generality of the people in England.——They (the parliament) no sooner met in 1649, but they ordered it to be hung up before their eyes, as a constant monitor to them ‡." " If all tables were as legible as those of the Lords and Commons, I believe their (*i e* subscribers of the covenant) number would be found more than a 4th part of the nation (in 1660, notwithstanding the death of perhaps more than one half of them from 1644 to 1660).. Can any considerate observer, take notice, that the covenant (in England) was imposed on, and submitted to, by all sorts and degrees of men in all counties, cities,

---

* Testimony. P. 20, 21, 22, 24. † P. 2.
‡ Covenanters Plea, P. 3, 70.

and

and towns, tendered, and since testified, by their public subscriptions, by the most of ministers in their several counties, and to their individual congregations, and yet without the supposal of a very great mortality, imagine not a fourth part of the nation (now living in 1660) to have taken it?——Nor shall I insist on the universal alacrity, joy and content of the most serious in England and Scotland, that accompanied the first making of the covenant, and the solemnities and order, in which it was taken in the city of London; and the several counties and congregations of England,—than which—no act ever passed among the people of England, more solemnly or more religiously.——The Solemn League and Covenant is really public and national (in England). (1.) Its matter is public and national, relating to the kingdom under its civil, religious and reformed capacity, being the reformation and defence of religion, under a national profession, and the honour and happiness of the king, privileges of the Parliament, and liberties of the subjects. (2.) These matters were consulted, debated and agreed to, by two distinct nations in their most public capacities. (4.) The end of it was public and national,—the *true liberty, peace, and safety of the kingdom*, wherein every one's private condition is included :——and that *the Lord may be one and his name one in the three kingdoms ; and the kingdoms of England and Scotland may remain conjoined in a firm peace to all posterity*,——in a case that concerned the good of these kingdoms (5.) The covenant was sworn by the nation. [1.] *Collectively*, in the most full and complete body, that could, or ever did represent the same, the Parliament consisting of Lords and Commons, and that in their public capacity, and with the greatest solemnity imaginable, did as the representative body of the kingdom, swear the covenant, which as a further testimony that it was a national covenant, they caused to be printed with their names subscribed, and to be hung up in all churches, and in their own (Parliament) House, as a compass, whereby to steer their debates, and to dictate unto all that should succeed them into that place and capacity, what obligations before God ly upon *the body of*

this

this nation. [2.] It was *universally* sworn by the people of this kingdom, (England) solemnly testified in their particular places of convention, all over the kingdom, and by all manner of persons, from eighteen years and upwards, and that at the command of, and by the authority of the Parliament, who, in their place, and in behalf of this nation, did order it to be *universally* sworn.—Certainly, whoever will but weigh the directions given and duly executed, in the tendering of the covenant in *all counties and parishes*, and taken by *all persons*, religious, military or civil.——If the several roils within the several parishes and precincts of this kingdom, in which the several names of such, as did swear the Solemn League and Covenant, were ingrossed, be viewed, it will be found that it was sworn by the *universality* of the nation; —and I hope we, who are a free people, tied by no bonds but such as we lay upon ourselves, may be allowed to bind ourselves by an oath. [3.] His Majesty (Charles II) did swear the Solemn League and Covenant, in behalf of himself and his successors, and that as King of Great Britain and Ireland.———More than six hundred ministers of England in thirteen different counties, in their testimonies, (1648) to the truths of Christ and to the Solemn League and Covenant, attest it as *national*.—The Yorkshire ministers say, " It cannot but be known to the churches abroad, that all the three kingdoms stand engaged by virtue of the Solemn League and Covenant *." The London ministers say, " We shall never forget, how solemnly and chearfully the *sacred* league was sworn,— wherein the three kingdoms stand engaged jointly and severally. The Parliament have not only enjoined it to be taken by all men above eighteen years of age, throughout the kingdom of England and dominion of Wales; but the Commons have also required it to be published on every monthly fast-day, for the better remembrance and observation of it, and that every congregation have one of the said Covenants fairly printed in a fair letter, in a table, fitted to hang

---

* Crofton's Peter's bonds abide, P 16, and Fastening of St. Peter's fetters, p. 108, 138,—146.

up in some public place of the Church, to be read †."

In IRELAND, Rutherford and his sixteen faithful brethren, who had full access to know the truth, affirm, That multitudes swore the solemn league. In Cox' history of Ireland, Ormond, then Lord lieutenant there, says, " The covenant hath been imposed by ordinance of (English) Parliament, (which hath the *supreme* power over Ireland as a dependent kingdom Act 6. Geo. I.)——The covenant was imposed on all that were under the power of the Parliament." In a subsequent page it is affirmed, That all the province of Ulster (in which the Protestants chiefly reside), and a considerable part of Munster were under the power of Parliament; and that in 1649, The Puritans and Presbyterians professed, that their regard to their covenant made them side with Charles II, against the Sectarians headed by Cromwel §." In the *Christian loyalty of the Presbyterians, particularly in Ulster, since their Settlement there by K James,*—the most of which is verified by original papers inserted, we have the following and like hints,—" The petition of *many thousand* Protestant inhabitants of Ulster presented to the English Parliament 1640, avows their approbation of the Scotch national covenant; and complain, that the Irish Prelates had exclaimed against it, and concurred with Lord lieutenant Strafford in imposing an oath, renouncing it;—The Scots, who were generally dissenters, *i. e. Presbyterians* took arms against the Popish *massacrers*, and were the first that appeared in Ulster against the common enemy, who were then exercising unheard of cruelty;—With the Scotch army of six thousand, under General Alexander Lesly, which were sent to check the ravage of the murderous Papists, ministers were sent to attend the several regiments, who, associating themselves with some formerly in Ireland, formed themselves into a Presbytery, in which Lesly and several other officers of the army, sit as ruling elders.—They preached both in camp and country.—At this time, those who

* Testim. P. 46. Paten's collect. of C n ess. p. 97.
§ Cox' hist. Vol. II. P. 177. 180, &c.

had fled from Ireland, on account of the oath imposed by Strafford, before the massacre begun, returned in great numbers, and joined with the Scotch army, and Sir John Clotworthy, a zealous puritan; so that he with his party scoured the whole county of Antrim *from massacring Papists*.——When the established (*i. e.* Episcopalian) clergy were generally destroyed by the massacre, or had fled, the work of the ministry was mostly in the hands of Presbyterians, who, with indefatigable industry, attended both camp and country, not without comfortable success.——In 1642, the Irish Protestants petitioned the Scotch General Assembly, that some ministers of the gospel might be sent to comfort them in their great calamity, when, by the massacre, left as without shepherds; and particularly that their own ministers, who had been formerly banished by Abp. Laud's partizans, might be restored to them.——Six ministers were sent to concur with those of the Scotch army sent thither by authority of king and Parliament; and as they came very seasonably to encourage the army and their friends, God mightily blessed their endeavours with success *." Upon a request of *very great numbers*, the Assembly 1643, sent them further supply of ministers.——A petition of the distressed Christians in the North of Ireland, subscribed by *very many hands* to the Assembly 1644, says,—" Your reward is with your God, for your zeal and care to have your reformation spread, in sending hither that blessed League and Covenant, which we much desired and longed for,—which hath had a wished and gracious success, by the blessing of God accompanying the pains of those, to whom the tendering of it was intrusted by you.——When the said —covenant was presented to the regiments (of your army) we made bold to lay hold on the opportunity, and *chearfully* and *unanimously* joined ourselves thereto, that, if we die (by the hand of the Popish murderers) we may die a covenanted people;" and they beg supply of ministers for twenty-four desolate congregations ‡ Much about the same time, " the English Parliament

* Christian Loyalty, &c. P. 137, 140, 175, 176, 87, 88.
‡ Acts of Ass. p. 151, 190, 191, 214,---217.

by an ordinance enjoined that covenant to be taken in Ireland; and accordingly it was sworn by almost all the Protestants in Ulster, who acknowledged the authority of the Parliament,——the greatest part of the Protestants in Ireland all concurred in it,—and their posterity enjoy large estates from that *English* Parliament which enjoined the taking of the covenant.——It known, that the Irish army under the Lord of Ards, were all Presbyterian covenanters.—Many of the Irish Protestants renewed the Solemn League about 1649; and hence the Presbytery of Bangor in their declaration that year affirm, " That they and others had *renewed* their covenant,—and warn, that none who had *renewed* covenant, should join the army of Ards, who, after he and they had *lately renewed* the covenant, had turned over to assist the malignants; and foretel that the quarrel of the covenant should pursue them,—as it soon did, in their ruin and of Ormond's army which they assisted.——The Irish Presbyterians, in their representation against the procedure of the Sectarians with K. Charles I, publicly read in their several congregations, avow the Solemn League, as *their covenant;* and warn the well affected to that covenant, to avoid all compliance with the Sectaries † The Presbyterian ministers in their Narrative to government of their stedfast loyalty, and of their sufferings under Cromwel, say, " We could not own them, *i. e* Cromwel and his *substitutes*, as lawful magistrates, and could not pray for their success, *&c.*—considering the strong obligation of the oath of God, that lay still upon us, to maintain His Majesty's power and greatness according to our covenant ‡."——Notwithstanding all the cruel banishment, imprisonment, *&c.* which they had suffered under Cromwel, for their attachment to K. Charles, there remained so many staunch covenanters in Ireland, that in one Synod of Bellimenoch, fifty-nine ministers, in 1662, refused to conform to Prelacy, which is more than were in some six Synods in Scotland. Nor, in any Synod here, except in that of Glasgow, which consists of a-

† Christian loyalty, P. 176, 177, 89, 143, 197,—200, 203
‡ Ibid. p. 214,—217.

bove 130 ministers, and in which the Protestors chiefly resided, was that number of Non-conformists exceeded [*]. From these hints it appears, that the body of Protestants in Ireland took the Solemn League and Covenant; and that the number of Covenanters there, could not be less than 50 or 60,000, if it was not double or triple that reckoning.

If then, Sir, the public engagements of representatives of Church and State can bind those represented by them and their posterity;—if the public engagements of parents can bind their descendents;—if the public engagements of the greater part of a society can bind the whole and their successors;—Our public covenants with God must bind the Protestants in Ireland, the whole nation of England, and in a peculiar manner the Scots, who are so manifestly affected by all the four sources of obligation, that no not our perjured Prelatists, for their own vindication, ever dared, that I know of, to contest it. And answerable to this source, these fourfold vows must fix upon us a kind of *fourfold solemn obligation to God*, frequently repeated, renewed, or confirmed: How fearful then must be our guilt, if we cast all the cords of God behind our back, in favours of gross heresy, blasphemy, idolatry, Popery!

4. Our ancestors did not covenant with God as mere individuals, but as a BODY. Covenanting at the same time with each other, they made a joint surrender of themselves to God. In their Bond of 1636, they call it a blessed and loyal *conjunction*. In their Reasons against giving it up, they call it a *Bond of union and conjunction,—a mutual union and conjunction* amongst themselves; and in reasons of protestation they call it a bond of *inviolable union* amongst themselves [‡]. The Assembly August 6th, 1649, say,—" Our engagement therein is not *only national*, but personal."—The subject bound by the covenant being thus, not merely particular persons, but a church and nation, the obligation of it must be as permanent as the society bound by it.

[*] Wodrow's hist. Vol. I. p. 155. Appendix, p. 78.
[‡] Stevenson, p. 345, 354.

5. Our

5. Our anceſtors did what they could to make their covenant as binding as poſſible. The expreſs terms in which the different forms of it are conceived, manifeſt it a *promiſe*, an *oath*, a *vow*, a *covenant*. If then there be any *binding force* in a promiſe from the *truth of men* which is therein pledged; if there be any *religion* in an oath becauſe of the *reverence* we owe to the ſacred name of God interpoſed in it; if any *obligation* reſults from a vow, becauſe of the *fealty* we thereby owe to God; if a man be *obliged* to keep his covenant from regard to *truth or juſtice* due to others, who are parties in it;—all theſe, tranſacted with the utmoſt ſolemnity, muſt concur in conſtituting the *binding force* of this *public engagement*.—Hence the Commiſſion 1651, in their Warning, ſay, " The *bonds and obligations* that lie upon us to this duty, by the law of God, the law of nature and the National Covenant and Solemn League, and the pains therein contained, whereunto we have devoted ourſelves, if we ſhall deſert or fail *."

6 Our anceſtors plainly intended, that their public covenants ſhould bind all future generations. In 1638, they lamented their own ſins as breaches of the covenant made or renewed in 1581, 1590, 1596 †. In their Reaſons againſt giving up their ſworn covenant, they affirm, " Our religious anceſtors, by the like oath, have obliged us to the ſubſtance and tenor of this.—This our oath being a religious and perpetual obligation, ſhould ſtand in vigour, for the more firm eſtabliſhment of religion in our own time, and in the *generations following*.—Although the innovations of religion were the occaſion of the making of this covenant, yet our intention was againſt theſe and all other innovations and corruptions, to eſtabliſh religion by an *everlaſting covenant, never* to be forgotten §." In their preamble to the covenant that year, they ſay, " Being convinced in our own minds, and profeſſing

---

* Stevenſon, P. 10.

† Hiſt. Mot. p. 43. Short Relat. on 1638. Aſſ. Letter to Helvetians. Steven. p. 285. Bail. Let. p. 35. Apol. Relat. p. 47. Wilſon's defence, p. 237, 238, 242, &c.

§ Stevenſon, p. 347, 348, 351.

with

with our mouths, that the *present* and *succeeding* generations are bound to keep the foresaid national oath and subscription (of 1581, 1590, 1596) inviolable." In the Solemn League, they swear, " We shall endeavour that these kingdoms may remain conjoined in a firm peace and union to *all posterity*."

7. The ends of these covenants declared in their express words are *perpetual* till the end of time, viz. " To maintain the true worship of God, the majesty of our king, and the peace of the kingdom, for the common happiness of ourselves and *our posterity,—* that religion and righteousness may flourish in the land to the glory of God, &c ‡." " To promote the glory of God, and the advancement of the kingdom of our Lord Jesus Christ,—the honour and happiness of the King's Majesty, and his *posterity*, and the public liberty, safety, and peace of the kingdoms ; that we and our posterity may, as brethren, live in faith and love, and the Lord delight to dwell in the midst of us ;—that the Lord may be one and his name one in the three kingdoms,—may turn away his wrath, and establish these churches and kingdoms in peace §."

If then, the matter being moral duty, was proper for a covenant of perpetual obligation ; if the covenanters had full power to bind the whole society and their posterity; if the subject upon which the obligation was laid be permanent ; if the end of the covenanters and their covenant was to fix the obligation upon posterity, as well as upon the immediate engagers ; and if they did every thing in their power to render that obligation solemn and permanent, What further evidence of the perpetuity of that obligation can any man demand, who singly regards the honour of God, or the welfare of this church and nation ? May I therefore adopt the words of a truly great man, " It was the glory of Scotland, that we were solemnly in covenant with God,—wherein our forefathers, for themselves engaged and swore against *Popery*, Prelacy, superstition, and every thing contrary to the word of God ;—and to the doctrine, worship, discipline and government of the reformed church of Scotland,

---

‡ Covenant of 1638.   § Covenant of 1643.

and

and that as we should answer to Jesus Christ at the great day, and under the pain of his everlasting wrath;——May not our hearts bleed to think on our defection from old covenanted principles, and our violation of our engagements, yea of the burning and burial of our covenants,—and the prevalence of *abjured Popery* in this land.——*Covenant-obligation* to duty is what we still stand under,—though many be ashamed and refuse to own these obligations,—the glory of our land.——Let us go forward—lamenting our sinful defection from a covenanted reformation, and acknowledging our solemn *covenant-obligation* †.——Never was a nation more solemnly bound to the Lord by national covenants. Religious covenants in scripture comprehend absent as well as present, and posterity to come as well as the covenanting forefathers, Deut. xxix. 14, 15, 22, 24, 25. Now, our solemn covenants, which our forefathers entered into, being nothing but a *super-added* and accumulative obligation, to what we were previously bound to by the word of God, they cannot but stand binding upon us their posterity §.——As Israel avouched the Lord to be their God by solemn covenants, that were binding upon them and their posterity after them ; so in this moral duty, We, in our forefathers, followed the example,—entering into a solemn covenant with him, which he many signal ways countenanced,—attended with internal displays of (his) power and glory.——To disparage these covenants is to cast dung upon our glory. I think it worse than the breaking, burning, and burying of them. To bespatter their reputation, and deny their obligation, is to render them odious to all generations ‡.——There is—a *superadded obligation* lying on us by our covenants of gratitude and duty, which, though it bind us to nothing, but what we were authoritatively bound to before, yet it strengthens the obligation ++.——When God hath manifested his covenant of grace to a people, receiving them to be his people, and they thereupon have entered into a covenant of duty with him, avouching him to be their God, and promising thro'

† R. Erskine's works fol. Vol. I, p. 62. § Ibid, p. 170, 304.
‡ Ibid. p. 489. ++ Ibid. Vol. II, p. 224.

grace,

grace, subjection to him, though it were four hundred, yea four thousand years, it stands; and they who succeed are bound by the covenant.——A number of honest covenanters, when they avouched the Lord to be their God, and promised obedience to him, did it in the faith of his avouching them to be his people, and trusting to his covenant of grace and promise, and not to their covenant or engagement. We, in these lands, have devoted ourselves to the Lord, in which we were warranted by many scripture precedents——Never was an action done more sedately and advisedly.—The binding obligation of it upon us is plain. If we have the benefit of that religion to which our forefathers swore, we must be heirs of that oath they came under to the Most High (as Levi paid tithes in his father's loins, so we, in our forefathers, swore to this covenant). We are obliged to stand to it, though it were never so many years after.——Being partakers of the benefit, we are bound to do that which they promised to do for it. If a parent bind his children, are not their seed and heirs bound by his promise as well as they were? What continual changes and confusions would there be in the world, if persons themselves were only to be tied by their own personal bonds?—How much more impiety is it for men, to deny that *obligation by covenant to God*, made by their forefathers in their name.—— Our solemn covenants, are one of the grounds of our claim to him,---and of his continuing his claim to us, who own these covenants.---How will God avenge the violation of a lawful oath, made with himself in this land?---Unless these professed Presbyterians can now prove, that *Presbytry is sinful*, they must acknowledge that our national covenants are binding on us in this matter.—If a covenant in things lawful be not binding, then no covenant ever was §.

§ R. Erskine's works, Vol. II. p. 142, 224, 104. Comp. Hind let loose, p. 514.—— 521. Apol. Relat. p. 227,---416. Discourse at the renewing of the covenants, 1688. M'Ward's earnest contendings. p. 229,---230, 266. Examinat. of 13. Bp. Leighton's Accomodation. English ministers testimonies to Solemn League. Covenanters plea, Crofton's tracts on covenant. &c. &c.

OBJECT.

OBJECT. I. "Many things were wrong in the imposing and taking of these covenants; and their words are ill chosen, as to *extirpate* Popery, Prelacy, *i.e.* to kill Papists and Prelatists." ANSW. (1) Let us allow no malignant enemy or perjured violator of these covenants to be held a sufficient witness against them. Nor let us have the long ago refuted calumnies of such men revived upon their mere authority. (2) Though the covenant had had infirmities, even infirmities sufficient to have hindered the swearing of it, as the Doctors of Aberdeen and Oxford pretended, was the case,—it may nevertheless bind when once it is sworn. Though its matter had been in part sinful and self-contradictory, it would bind to the part which was lawful.——Though the authority which imposed it, had been insufficient, and the manner of imposing it improper, it would bind when once sworn. Zedekiah was in some respect compelled to swear allegiance to Nebuchadnezzar, whose sovereignty over Judah was very disputable, yet his oath bound him, Ezek. xvii. 12,—19. 2 Chron. xxxvi. 13.——Though our covenanters ends had been carnal, or even sinful, the oath, as far as lawful in its matter, is binding, when once it is sworn.——Without allowing these things as *fixed principles*, no oaths or covenants could be any securities among mankind. (3) If Popery and Prelacy be plants which God hath not planted, why may we not, as lawfully, in our stations, endeavour to *extirpate* or *root* them out, as we may mortify the deeds of our body, that we may live? The one includes no more violence against mens persons than the other, Rom. viii. 13. Do you imagine, that the covenanters swore to cut their own throats, or tear out their own hearts, when they engaged to endeavour, in their station, to extirpate *every thing contrary to the power of godliness*, as indwelling sin, vain thoughts, &c. which adhere to believers in this life, certainly are.

OBJECT. II. "Many in England and Ireland never took the Solemn League, or took it in a sense consistent with Prelacy or Independency." ANSW. I do not expect that any hater of that covenant will ever be able to invalidate the proof which hath been given of the of the covenanters in both these kingdoms. (2) The covenanters declared "that an oath is to be taken in the plain sense of the words, without equivocation or mental reservation.—It cannot bind to sin; but in any thing not sinful, being taken, it binds to performance, although to a man's own hurt *." All but Jesuits profess the same principle. And indeed if oaths, vows, or covenants bind not men, according to the plain meaning of their words, they become quite useless. Mens prevarication therefore, in favours of Prelacy or Independency, cannot free them from the obligation of an oath, which strikes against both. (3) As the Scots stood bound by their National Covenant to every duty contained in the Solemn League, long before the English had a thought of covenanting along with them, and did also swear the solemn league, no neglect or prevarication of either English or Irish can free us from our obligation. It was neither to the English nor to the Irish, but chiefly to the faithful and unchangeable God of all grace, that our fathers bound themselves and their seed. The Assembly in their *Letter to the council of London*, justly observe, "It is not in the power of any human authority to absolve you from adhering to this so solemnly sworn League and Covenant." And in another letter, "The covenant hath been broken by many in both kingdoms. —We do not doubt, but there are *many seven thousands* in England, who have retained their integrity in that business." And in their *Warning* 1648, "The violation of the covenant by some in England doth not set us free from the obligation of it. No laws, nor authority on earth can absolve us from so solemn an obligation to the Most High.—We are not acquitted from the obligation of our solemn covenants because of the troubles.—In the worst of times, all those duties whereunto by covenant, we oblige ourselves, do still ly upon us.—We have sworn, and we must perform it." And in their *Warning* 1649, "Albeit the League and Covenant be despised by that prevailing party in England, yet the obligation of that covenant is *perpetual*; and all the duties contained therein

---

* Confession of Faith, chap. XXII. 4.

therein are conſtantly to be minded aud proſecuted, by every one of us and our *poſterity*, according to their place and ſtation." And in their *Letter to brethren in England*, " Although there were none in the one kingdom, who did adhere to the covenant, yet were not the other kingdom, nor any perſon in either of them, abſolved from the bond thereof; ſince in it, we have not only ſworn by the Lord, but alſo covenanted with him. It is not the failing of one or more that can abſolve others from their duty or TIE to him. Beſides, the duties therein contained being in themſelves lawful, and the grounds of our TIE thereto moral, though others forget their duty, yet doth not their defection free us from that obligation which lies upon us by the covenants, in our places and ſtations. The covenant being intended as one of the beſt means of ſtedfaſtneſs, it were ſtrange to ſay, that the backſlidings of any ſhould abſolve others from the TIE thereof, eſpecially ſeeing our engagement therein is *not only national*, but *perſonal*.—All theſe kingdoms joining together to aboliſh that oath by law, could not diſpenſe therewith, much leſs can any one of them, or any party in either do the ſame.——(They are) teſtimonies which the Lord Chriſt hath entred as proteſtations, to preſerve his right in theſe ends of the earth, long ago given unto him for his poſſeſſion, and of late confirmed by ſolemn covenant."

OBJECT. III. " The influence of the Highland chiefs, and the groſs ignorance of the Scotch iſlands, together with the general diſlike of the covenant at the Reſtoration and Revolution, are *internal evidences*, that but a part, perhaps a ſmall part, of the Scots took the covenant." ANSW. I boldly defy you to invalidate the proofs I have brought to the contrary. Nay, for ought I know, you cannot produce one of theſe perjured Prelatiſts, that pretended that only the ſmaller part of the Scotch nation took the covenant, eſpecially in 1590, 1638, & 1643. (2.) Were the Highland chiefs, and the groſs ignorance of the iſlanders, occaſioned by the negligence of the curates, a whit more able to withſtand the enlightening and heart-bowing power of God, ſo remarkably manifeſted on theſe occaſions, than K. Charles and many others on the continent ? Have we not produced evidence that multitudes of the Highlanders entered into the reformers covenant, 1638, and were not Argyle, Mar, and many other Highland chiefs zealous covenanters ? Did not such as were otherwise minded take the covenant of 1581, as imposed by the Privy council according to its original meaning ? Did not even the Doctors and Prelatic inhabitants of Aberdeen take that bond, without approving the council's limitation of it to its original meaning ? (3) You can produce no evidence that the covenanting work was not carried on in the Scotch islands, but such as we have, that never a Hebrew child was circumcised on the 8th day, from Isaac to John Baptist ;—or that never a weekly Sabbath was observed from the creation till the manna fell around the Hebrew camp, *i. e.* want of positive evidence to the contrary,—and that too in places, of which, to this moment, we have little account, except what relates to their situation, soil, product, or the like. (4.) It is highly absurd to pretend, that the so general disregard of the covenants, twelve or forty years after the last taking of them, is *internal evidence* that few had taken them. Will it irrefragably prove, that Adam was never made after the image of God, or taken into covenant with him, because within a few days or hours he had become a sinner, hating both God and his covenant,—or that devils were never created holy and happy, because within a few days they had left their first estate ? Will the general concurrence of the Hebrews in worshipping the golden calf, prove that they had not entered into solemn covenant with God, about forty days before ? Will their subsequent apostasies, prove that but few of them had covenanted with God, under Joshua, Asa, Joash, Hezekiah, Josiah, Ezra and Nehemiah ? Will Peter's fearfully heinous and repeated denial of Christ, prove that he had not, a few hours before, solemnly engaged against it ?

OBJECT. IV. " Force or fear caused many to covenant." ANSW. Though force or fear should have rendered the manner of covenanting unacceptable to God, they cannot render void an oath which is sworn. (2.) I will never contend, that the penalty annexed by
law

law to the refusal of the covenant in 1643, or even on some other occasions, was proper. But, after a laborious search, I find no proper evidence, that any force was ever used in Scotland to make any take the covenant, except in 1639, by Montrose and Monro, two military men, without any warrant from either church or state,—the former, if not both of whom afterward turned out a malignant murderer of his covenanting brethren. Never, Sir, pick up or retail the mere inventions of perjured violators of these covenants, who were glad to say any thing to conceal or excuse their own wickedness. (3.) In 1638, when the covenanting was most universal, the bishops and some other anticovenanters, afraid of prosecution for their enormous debts, or for their oppressive and other wicked deeds,—and perhaps chiefly to calumniate the covenanters at court, did flee their country. But none were obliged to do so for refusing the covenant. Fear of danger probably restrained some from reviling a Bond which the nation so highly esteemed. But none, that I know of, were thereby constrained to swear it. Some mobs happened, occasioned by the king's suspension of the common exercise of the civil law, and the sitting of its courts. But these were detested by the zealous covenanters, and not one of them appears either to have been intended, or to have issued in favours of the covenant. If the influences of God's Spirit, and the affecting appearances of his Providence—as at Sinai or in the apostolic age, awed or allured numbers to take the covenant whose hearts were not sincere before him,—should we quarrel with the Almighty on that account?——But, Sir, Henderson, Dickson, and Cant, who being the principal leaders of the covenanting work that year, affirm to the doctors of Aberdeen, who were eager to have detected them of falsehood, if it had been possible, " No pastors in our knowledge have been either forced to flee or have been threatened with the want of their stipends for refusing their subscription; but some have of their own accord, gone to court for procuring protection against their creditors,—and have made lies between the king and his people. Others have wilfully refused to abide with their flocks, for no reason, but because the people

have

have subscribed.—Arguments have been taken from (promised) augmentation of stipends to hinder subscription. Fear of worldly loss rather hinders men to subscribe, than scruples of conscience.—The prelates flight seems rather to have proceeded from inward furies of accusing consciences, &c.——In this day of the Lord's power, his people have *most willingly offered* themselves in multitudes like the dew of the morning. Others, of no small note, have offered their subscriptions, and have been refused till time should try their sincerity, from love to the cause, and *not from the fear of man.* No threatenings have been used, except of the deserved judgments of God, nor force, except the force of reason from the high respects which we owe to religion, to our king, to our native country, to ourselves, and to our posterity *." (4.) Since the covenanting work was so remarkably countenanced by the Holy Ghost,—attended with perhaps more sincere mourning for sin,—more serious repentance and solid conversion to God, than hath within an equal space of time and place, happened any where in the world, since the apostolic age,—and since the covenanters in their vow deponed, that they covenanted *without any worldly respect or inducement*, as far as human infirmity would allow,——Take heed, Sir, lest after your objection hath manifested the carnality, selfishness, and dissimulation of your own religious appearances —God, at last, should publicly expose you as a blasphemer of his great work, and a malicious slanderer of his people, as *wilfully perjured*.

OBJECT. V. " It is impossible our covenanters could understand their bonds, particularly in that which relates to Popery in the *national covenant*, or to prelacy in the *solemn league*." ANSW. Ignorance indeed hinders a right and acceptable swearing of oaths or covenants, but cannot invalidate their binding force if once they be sworn; otherwise millions in Britain would,

---

* Answers to doctors of Aberdeen, P. 42, 44.
The General Assembly 1649, in their act, Sef. 19th, appear so far from forcing men into their covenant, that they earnestly enjoin and appoint the utmost caution to be used for preventing such persons taking of it as did not sincerely approve it, and resolve to prosecute the ends of it.

through ignorance, be freed from all their solemn engagements in Baptism and the Lord's supper; and thousands freed from all obligation of their oaths of allegiance or fidelity to magistrates; or even their oaths to declare the truth and nothing else, in witness bearing. Candidates for the ministry needed but keep themselves in a great measure ignorant of the doctrines of the Confession of Faith and duties of the ministerial office, in order to render their ordination vows or subscriptions *altogether unobligatory*. (2.) Being trained up in the abominations of popery or prelacy, or having frequent access to witness them, our covenanting ancestors, who had common sense, might have more knowledge of them, than most clergymen in Scotland now have; even as a common sailor, who hath served 20 years in a man of war, may have more knowledge of her tackling and other pertinents, than all the learned doctors of six British universities.

OBJECT. VI : " If nothing be engaged to in these covenants, but what God hath declared or required in his word, they *never could lay any obligation* upon the covenanters, much less a perpetual obligation upon their posterity : It is absolutely inconsistent with sound philosophy, Christianity or common sense to imagine that any human deed can bind to any thing declared in the word, or required by the law of God." ANSW 1. Then it seems the common Protestant doctrine of our Confession of Faith, which in your ordination vows you solemnly declared to be *founded on the word of God*, viz. *That a man* BINDS HIMSELF *by oath to what is* GOOD *and* JUST, *that in* ANY THING *not sinful, it* BINDS *to performance*; That by a vow we *more strictly* BIND OURSELVES TO NECESSARY DUTIES, &c. must be grossly erroneous. (2) Instructed by some Papist or some ring-leader in the perjurious violation of these covenants in the last century, you have indeed now hit upon a sentiment, which if proven, would effectually undermine the obligation of our covenants, and for ought I know, all religion,—all morality,—all mutual trust and order among mankind along with it. If our promises, oaths, vows or covenants can have no *binding force* except in things to which the revelation and law of God cannot reach;

neither

neither Adam, nor Christ as Mediator, could bind themselves to fulfil God's law; and so there must be no proper, no real covenant of works or of grace; and so no religion among mankind. And, for the same reason, the promises of God, in so far as their matter corresponds to his natural excellencies can have *no binding* force; and thus the foundation of our faith and hope is quite overturned. All engagements in Baptism or the Lord's Supper to believe what God reveals, receive what he offers, and do what he commands, must be absolutely *null and void*, destitute of all *binding force*.——Jesuitical equivocation and mental reservation are no more necessary in the making of promises, covenants or vows, or in swearing promissory oaths of allegiance, fidelity or witness bearing; or in subscribing Articles, Creeds or Confessions of Faith, Calls to ministers, Bonds or Bills of service or debt.——If the law of God, which is exceeding broad can but reach to the matter of them, and require the believing, maintaining or practising of what is therein engaged, that alone renders them *null and void, and not binding* to all intents and purposes. And so there can be no such a thing as *perjury, perfidy*, or *breach of promise*, except it be with respect to such things as the law of God could not directly or indirectly reach,—which if it be as perfect and exceeding broad as the Bible affirms, must certainly be very few and very trifling;—for *where there is no law,*-no binding of a law,-*there can be no transgression*.——Mens promises, covenants, oaths and vows, in word or writ, in so far as they respect things to which the law of God can reach, must be mere *villainous impositions*, seeming *to bind*, while they do not, in the smallest degree; and therefore ought to be detested, instead of being required, made, or trusted.——For the same reason, no commands of parents, masters, magistrates, or any other superiors being *human deeds*, can have any *binding force* in any thing relative to religion, equity, kindness, &c. to which the law of God can reach its requirements, and hence cannot be *lawfully* OBEYED, or their authority regarded, except when they commend what is *absolutely indifferent and trifling*.——If human engagements and commands can only bind men to that which

is

is *absolutely indifferent,* it is plain, that we can only be answerable to men for such parts of our conduct as the law of God did not reach;—but, let men once firmly believe, that their promises, covenants, oaths or vows, and the commands of superiors, have *no binding force,* but in that which is left absolutely indifferent by the law of God; and that they are answerable to men only for such parts of their conduct as the law of God could not reach,—how naturally they will rush headlong into all manner of profligacy, every man doing that which is right in his own eyes, in every thing important. (3.) How absurd to pretend honouring of religion, or of the law of God by making it the murderer of that *deputed authority* which God hath, by it, granted to men; or of these covenants, oaths or vows, which He hath therein appointed as means of his worship.—Not only scripture, but even common sense dictates, that the authority of God in his law cannot be rightly regarded, unless in a way of also regarding that authority which he hath deputed to men, and all the commands or self engagements which proceed from it, in due subordination to it. If I read my Bible daily, in obedience to the command of God as my God in Christ,—in obedience to Christ as appointed by God to be my mediatorial prophet and king,—and at the same time in due subordination hereto,—in obedience to my civil ruler, as the minister of God for good to men,—in obedience to my pastor or church judicature as the messenger of Christ to me,—in obedience to my parents or masters as God's deputy-governors over me,—and in fulfilment of the vow, which I as God's deputy-governor over myself, have laid myself under, according to his appointment, Where is the inconsistency? Must I wickedly put asunder the *immediate* and *deputed* authority of God, which he hath so closely and delightfully joined together? God forbid.

OBJECT. VII. "What have we to do with our father's engagements in religion, to which we never gave any personal consent, especially after we have become capable to judge and choose for ourselves,—nay to do with engagements, which I cannot prove my ancestors ever took." ANSW. (1.) To rest obligation to pay debt or perform duty, on the *debtor's* proving the contraction of it, or engagement to it, is highly absurd

surd in itself, and opens a wide door for breaking through almost every engagement. According to this scheme you may hold your ancestors, who lived 130 years ago unbaptized Heathens, and perhaps yourself too, and so renounce your baptism, because you *cannot prove* that ever you received it. If God, who is our *creditor* in these covenants, can prove our ancestors taking of them, he will hold us bound by their deed; and even though they did not take them, he will hold us bound by the deed of the society and its representatives. (2.) You know, that Lord ———, about four hundred years ago, granted your ancestor, the valuable estate of ———, to be held under him and his heirs, for a very small honorary service, as an acknowledgment of vassalage; and that the celebrated farmer *A. B.* about six years ago took a ninety-nine years lease of one of your farms at a very high rent. Have you certified the present heirs of that Lord and Farmer, That they are no-wise bound by their progenitors deeds, unless they have given their own personal consent,—and that the one may recal your estate, and the other may keep your farm, and refuse to pay you any rent?——You have not, nor ever will You allow such freedoms only to be used with God,—not with yourself;—too strong a presumption, That you more value your estate and rent, than all that you hold of God in religion, and all the honour you owe to him. (3.) If our fathers bound us to any thing in religion which is not warranted by the word of God, we have nothing to do with it, but to bewail their sin in such engagement. But, if they bound us to what is commanded by the law of God, we must stand bound,—till we prove from scripture, that vows binding to duty are not lawful; or that fathers have no right to devote their children to Gods service. No slothful or wilful ignorance or withholding of personal consent, can so much as excuse the non-performance of such engagements. Nothing can free from their *binding force*, which would not annul our baptismal vows. (4) Once more, Sir, be pleased to review these public covenants of our fathers, in their principal contents and meaning. They were a *solemn acquiescence* in and *confirmation* of God's grant of the utmost ends of the earth to his Son Jesus Christ for his possession, fion. They implied a *solemn acceptance* of God himself in Christ as the God, Saviour and portion of the covenanters and their posterity freely granted to them in the gospel,—and of his oracles and ordinances as the means of familiar fellowship with Him,—a *resolution* through his grace to retain him and them, as their inestimable privileges,—and a *solemn engagement*, thankfully to improve these privileges in an holy obedience to all his commandments, to promote his glory, and the temporal, spiritual and eternal advantage of these covenanters and their seed. Now, Sir, do you so heartily envy our Redeemer his Father's grant of the ends of the earth for his possession, Psal. ii. 8. that you would gladly renounce our ancestors solemn acquiescence in it? Do do you so heartily dislike the having of a reconciled God in Christ for your and your posterity's God, Saviour and portion, and his pure oracles and ordinances for your privileges, that you would fondly renounce a solemn acceptance of God's gracious grant of them sealed and confirmed by the remarkable influences of his Spirit? Do you so undervalue these enjoyments, and hate a grateful and self-profiting obedience to all the commandments of God, that you would gladly renounce a solemn obligation to it? Or, are you offended with the declared ends of these covenants, *viz.* the glorifying of God, the preservation and reformation of religion and promoting the welfare of the nation,—and that God may delight to dwell among us to the latest posterity?—You will perhaps pretend, that you love our reformed doctrine, worship, Presbyterian government and discipline: but hate to be bound to them, especially by others than yourself. But, Sir, for the same reason you must renounce your baptismal engagements, and state your quarrel with God himself, who hath appointed vows, as his ordinance for hedging up men to their duty, and who hath entered into covenants with parents for their posterity as well as for themselves. Moreover, it is scarce credible, that you can love every thing engaged to in a vow, and yet hate to be bound by it, after God hath signally countenanced it. It is scarce possible, that my wife can dearly love her husband, and the order and enjoyments of my family, if she hate and will to renounce her marriage Vow.

FINIS.

Books Sold by JOHN BRYCE, at his Shop opposite to Gibson's-Wynd, Salt-market, either in Wholesale or Retail.

BOOKS IN FOLIO.

I. HENRY's Commentary, on the old and new testament 6 vols, large print. Price £ 3-10-0.

II. A body of divinity, wherein the doctrines of the Christian Religion are explained and defended; being the substance of several lectures on the Assembly's larger Catechism. In one volume. By Thomas Ridgley, D. D. late dissenting minister in London. Price 11s and 6d.

III. The Christian in complete armour, or a treatise of the saints war with the devil, by William Gurnal, M. A. Price 10s.

IV. Josephus' whole works Price 11s.

V. Clark's martyrology. Price 9s and 6d.

VI. Henry's practical works, half bound. Price 4s

BOOKS IN QUARTO.

VII. An exposition of the epistle to the Romans, with large practical observations. by the reverend Mr John Brown, sometime minister of the Gospel at Rotterdam in Holland. Price 7s.

VIII. Willison's whole works Price 7s.

BOOKS IN OCTAVO.

IX. Mr Ralph Erskine's practical works, 10 vols. Price £ 1-8-0.

X. The works of the late reverend Mr Robert Traill, minister of the Gospel at London, 3 vols, price 6s.

XI. Religious cases of conscience answered in an evangelical manner, by S. Pike and S. Hayward, to which is now added, not in any former edition, the Spiritual Companion, or the professed Christian tried at the bar of God's word; being some pious thoughts in answer to thirty practical questions, of equal importance with the above cases.--- Together with some free thoughts on the character of the happy man. Price 2s and 6d

XII. Familiar Letters on a variety of religious subjects, by Jonathan Dickinson, A. M President of the College of New-Jersey. Price 2s.

XIII. Christ crucified; or the marrow of the Gospel evidently held forth in seventy-two Sermons on the whole fifty-third chapter of the prophecy of Isaiah, by Mr James Durham, sometime minister of the gospel in Glasgow. Price 2s and 6d.

XIV. The unsearchable riches of Christ, and of grace and glory in and thro' him, in fourteen communion Sermons by Mr James Durham, sometime minister of the Gospel in Glasgow. Price 1s and 3d.

XV. A practical exposition of the 130th Psalm, by John Owen, D. D. Price 2s and 6d.

XVI Christ the righteousness of his people; or the doctrine of justification by faith in him represented in several sermons preached at Pinner's-hall, London, by Mr. Richard Raw- price 1s 6d

www.ingramcontent.com/pod-product-compliance
Lightning Source LLC
Chambersburg PA
CBHW030312170426
43202CB00009B/975